The Mammoth Book of
PUZZLES

compiled by
Victor Serebriakoff

Also available by Victor Serebriakoff

The Mammoth Book of
PUZZLES

compiled by
Victor Serebriakoff

ROBINSON
London

Constable Publishers
3 The Lanchesters,
162 Fulham Palace Road
London W6 9ER
www.constablerobinson.com

First published in the UK by Robinson
an imprint of Constable & Robinson Ltd. 1992

A copy of the British Library Cataloguing in
Publication Data is available from the British Library.

ISBN 1–84119–353–4

Printed and bound in the EU

INTRODUCTION
by David J. Bodycombe

This remarkable book contains IQ puzzles and quizzes of every description. Codes, crosswords and anagrams await the word fans among you. Mathematical brains will look forward to the series and combinatory problems. In addition to the illustrated technological challenges, there are a goodly number of varied visual-spatial puzzles. And who doesn't enjoy a quiz? – for there are several of those too.

One of my personal favourite types of puzzle are those that appear normal but in fact lateral thought is necessary to arrive at the right answer. "Catch question" is not really the word for it, since this conjures up a very negative image in most people's minds. Victor invented a word for this category of question: the "Kickself". A puzzle which looks so difficult at first, but when you see the answer you just want to kick yourself. I think this fits the bill perfectly, and it's a term still used in Mensa's membership magazine to this day. These are puzzles at their best, and you can find a range of kickselfs throughout this book.

That's not to say that this book is only for IQ experts. Far from it. Victor has arranged these challenges so that – even if you don't make the grade on a particular task in one chapter – you are always learning new methods and experiences. Your chance of success improves as you progress. But next time the rules may be tweaked, so how are you going to cope? That is the crux of this book.

By organizing the subjects in a varied pattern, Victor Serebriakoff has set a challenge ahead which is deliberately designed so that you don't just play your strong suit and ignore the others. Use the whole brain approach to problem solving, and try not to rely on the logistical patterns that you may have seen before. Let me give you an analogy. When I hear people say, "Oh, I never enter competitions – I never win anything," I ask them how many competitions they actually enter. You can probably guess what their answer is. Likewise, don't fall into the trap of, "Oh, I can't solve that type of puzzle." Chances are you probably haven't tried that many. If the terrain becomes unfamiliar at any point, dig a little deeper and eventually the answers will present themselves to you. It might not happen on the first or second try, but remember that this bumper book provides all the practice you need to become an IQ mastermind.

Another feature I can recommend to you is the scoring and timing system, which adds a competitive element to the book. If you need a way of focusing the mind on the trials ahead, this is surely it. To my knowledge this is the only book that includes an ingenious IQ handicapping system. This is another way in which the author is saying to the reader: "Whether you are new to puzzles or an old hand, there are equal challenges here for you both."

Victor Serebriakoff was a remarkable man who I had the good fortune to meet on several occasions. His talents as a puzzle devisor, author, poet, technician, speaker and organizer are as varied and surprising as his own life story.

His surname originates from his Russian background which had links to the aristocracy, but Victor was born in 1912 in much poorer surroundings. His father was an immigrant manual worker and his London-born mother looked after his five siblings in the slums that formerly made up the East End of London. While teachers and fellow pupils at his school noticed his talents at an early age, somehow these were not recognised by Victor himself until much later. After school he became an office clerk in the timber firm where Vladimir, his father, worked – but his attention wandered and eventually he was sacked. A number of other menial jobs and periods of unemployment followed.

The call for conscription towards the end of World War II proved to be a wake-up call in more ways than one. Part of the assessment for the Army included a standardized intelligence test. At the age of 33, he had learnt for the first time – to his complete amazement – that his IQ was 161: that is, within the top 1% of the population. Rather than being sent to the front line, his intelligence – together with his love of reading and explaining concepts – earned him a role in teaching new recruits.

From there, his achievements were littered with "firsts". At the end of the War he turned down the offer of an Army commission and returned to the timber trade he knew so well. But instead of the menial tasks of the past, he rose to director level and modernized the business. He organized the business practices and instituted the use of the metric system years before other industries. He also invented a machine that graded the quality of the shape of timbers.

His greatest achievement, however, was his stewardship of the world-famous high-IQ organization Mensa. By all accounts, it had a difficult birth. Originally set up in 1946 by an Oxford postgraduate and an eccentric, wealthy lawyer, the "High IQ Club" – as it was then called – degenerated into an elitist mix of a black-tie dinner club and "think tank" group that did not find the ear of the Government. Furthermore the founders took it upon themselves to announce policies which were more their own pet beliefs rather than those held by the society's members. When Victor and his first wife, Mary, attended their first meeting in 1950, the total attendance was four – including themselves.

When one voice suggested that the society was nothing more than a meeting of friends and should be shut down, Victor – in his own, calmly quiet way – said "That would be a pity." Of course, the others saw their chance and immediately awarded him the roles of Secretary, Chief Executive and Principal Officer! Victor rose to the challenge, even though there were only 100 (mostly inactive) members and the grand sum of £56 in the bank account.

Victor's love of puzzles came from his ability to analyze a problem and propose a solution that would stand the test of time. How to rescue the society was a tough puzzle in itself, but he came up with the answer. The High IQ Club was now called Mensa, after the Latin word for "table". This reflected the wish for the society to become a "round table" organization with no individual setting the agenda. Victor encouraged debate amongst the members, but from now on Mensa itself was to hold no opinions. This is the way Mensa operates to this day.

He went on to add new energy to the organization – using marketing and media appearances to full effect. He played down the society's former aspirations as a think tank and instead built alliances with educational establishments. He also undertook the introduction of a proper supervised test as an entry requirement. Until this point, applicants had been offered membership based on a test taken at home, and it was not until Victor became Chairman that he found that the second-stage supervised test alluded to in the society's correspondence did not actually exist!

Victor's love of Mensa became literal in 1952. After his first wife died through illness, he sought the solace of a medical social worker called Winifred Rouse. As it happened, Victor had met her at previous Mensa meetings and – for reasons even he found hard to explain at the time – asked her out almost immediately. Their subsequent marriage lasted until her death in 1995.

Victor was made Honorary President of International Mensa in 1982 but, unlike former incumbents of the role, characteristically he took on an active role. Together with Dr Ware, credited as the society's original founder, Victor went on to build Mensa's international links – most notably setting up the office for Mensa in the USA. Today, the society has over 100,000 members in over 100 countries of the world. None of this would have been possible were it not for Victor's murmur comment of, "pity" all those years ago.

When you read through his own introduction in Chapter One, you will get a sense of Victor's sense of mischief. This was perfectly illustrated a few years ago when he wrote to Mensa's own members' magazine to say how much he hated it! And throughout his time with the organization he was constantly encouraging the membership to think about itself and what it should do as an entity. To assist this process, he devised a form of meeting called a "Think-In" where the speakers would be challenged to talk on a controversial topic while ensuring that their opinions were *new* and *true*.

The mischief of Serebriakoff continues within his puzzles. The puzzle setter needs to have a devious mind where – in some well-hidden back alley in the cerebellum – there lurks a slightly sadistic sense of humour. "They'll never get that," ponders the compiler's mind. And yet, at the end of the day the puzzle is there to be solved in the same way that a joke is set up to have a punch line. So while the devisor does everything in his power to tease you, they have their limits. Even Victor. Sometimes.

One suggestion for the more casual puzzlers among you: It can be surprising how people's approaches to problems vary. What seems like a ludicrous solution to one puzzler might seem obvious to another. So, if you wish, why not tackle these problems in tandem with a friend and see if two heads really are better than one.

To sum up then, perhaps Victor's constant quest for learning and his passion for mind play belie a gentleman who was young at heart. In fact, perhaps unlike some others of his generation, Victor had a great faith in youth. The housekeepers he employed when he lived alone were given opportunities usually not afforded to such a post, such as learning to use computers. He campaigned for educational improvements for gifted children. Even the original folios for this very book were put together with the help of schoolchildren.

Victor Serebriakoff died at home in Blackheath, London, on January 1, 2000 at the age of 87. To add to the significance, this was very close to the Greenwich Meridian. I know many people will mourn the departure of this great man. Although it will not make up for this loss, it's good to know that a little something of Victor's good humour and insatiable desire to challenge lives on in the form of this book.

I am delighted to reintroduce this classic collection of puzzles to a new audience, and I trust this is the beginning of many weeks of puzzling enjoyment.

David J. Bodycombe, 2001

PREFACE

How are we to understand the enormous market for puzzles and the hours we spend on them? This is the real puzzle. In a world full of real problems, we love to tussle and tease ourselves with hypothetical ones. My own answer is that puzzling is simply mental jogging, a way to keep your brain active, to stay young in mind, and for a time, Chrissakes!, to *know* the answer.

There is also a refreshment and attraction in problems that have a single unique and certain solution and no unknown negative side effects which all our real life problems seem to have. We turn away for a time from breaking our heads on our real problems, foggy and muddled as they are. They have too many unknowns and no true solution, only a 'best' one which we *always* find we have missed. It is with a sigh of relief that we escape to the clear and certain world of paper puzzles for a breather. I could amend the old 'paper doll' song thus – 'I'd rather have a paper quiz to really solve than just a fickle minded real-life plight'.

Rewarded by the little 'Eureka!' joy that comes with any solution, you'll remain mentally lithe and active – the better to tackle the real monsters that beset you – out there. I hope this Mammoth selection leaves you keen and sharp for that battle. Here they are – your half a thousand paper quizzes.

CHAPTER
ONE

I shall be frank. In the matter of puzzles, I confess I am a sadist. I am not ashamed. I glory in it. I caused widespread misery by writing my *FIRST* and then my even more evil *SECOND MENSA PUZZLE BOOK* (different titles in USA). They were fiendishly and cruelly difficult and perplexing. Then, not satisfied with adding many more torturing problems to a world where there is no shortage of them, I wrote what purported to be a novel, called *"My Alien Self"*. It was, when opened, a puzzle book in disguise with the diabolical riddles slyly woven into the text.

Now, angrily finding that there are other puzzles abroad which are even more subtly teasing and frustrating than mine, I have set out to build up this collection of the worst horrors and foist it on unsuspecting puzzlers everywhere. I know that most puzzle addicts are masochistically hooked on their wretched torment. Nyeh! nyeh! You cannot help yourselves.

I shall show no mercy. I am making new, harsh demands on my readers. For the first time, there is a strict time allowance for each puzzle. You will be fighting the clock all the way to gain a less than shameful number of merit points as you go through this mammoth collection. There will be no slack and sloppy puzzling at any old pace which other puzzle setters allow. This job has been work studied, and a proper rate of progress is required.

And I am sadistically pleased with another idea. Handicapping. Another first. I am not going to let the clever puzzler exploit a genetic and/or environmental advantage. Puzzlers are going to be handicapped. Mensa types will be clobbered. I was inspired by an SF novel, in which those of higher intelligence had, like handicapped racehorses, weights chained to their bruised and straining bodies – just to even things up a bit. This was done in the name of Equality and so it shall be with you, my readers, my victims. First you take an IQ test, and this sets your handicap. The hard-earned merit points you gain as you labour on through hundreds of tough puzzles will be reduced in proportion to your IQ. Most puzzlers are honest. What is the sense in cheating yourself? So I am relying on you to keep to my cruel rules.

HERE IS HOW IT WORKS

First you do the preliminary IQ test, find your score, and make a note of it.

Then there are 26 chapters of mixed puzzles, about 15 to each, about an evening of intense thinking for an average puzzler in each chapter. Each puzzle has a time limit. You solve the puzzle, and write your answer in the space provided. If you solve it in less than the allotted number of minutes, you may credit your running total with the minutes (merit points) gained. Work to the nearest minute (5 minutes 31 seconds counts as 6 minutes, 5 min 29 secs = 5 minutes). If you exceed the time allowance but do, against the odds, actually solve a puzzle, you will get five points only for all your labour.

There is an answer page at the end of each chapter, where you record your gain and running total as you labour on. THERE WILL BE NO POINTS FOR INCORRECT ANSWERS but, reluctantly, no penalties for overtime solutions.

When, if ever, you reach the end, you come to the reckoning. Your total score for the whole book is subject to a handicap adjustment according to IQ. First you add 2 noughts to your score. Sounds good! It is not. Then you divide the new total by your IQ which will, for most puzzlers, be over 120, even if it is not up to the Mensa level of 130 (the one-in-fifty level).

INTELLIGENCE TESTS

Your intelligence quotient (IQ) is a rough and ready measure of how intelligent you are. How good you are at logic, verbal comprehension, and handling symbolic knowledge. IQ tests are fixed so that the average score of the whole population works out at about 100. A score of 70 on a test valid for your own culture would indicate a feeble mind, and a score of 130 or so (depending on the test) would put you in the Mensa class. You'd be on what is statistically called the 98th percentile, that is you would come in the top two percent of the population for cleverness. I am not too keen on IQ as a measure myself. I prefer the percentile rating which can be deduced from IQ.

Your percentile rating tells you where you stand in your cultural group as to how your mind copes with logical and mathematical problems, how difficult the ideas you can grasp, and how good your judgement is. If you are on the 50th percentile you are average, 50% of folk would score lower than you at the test. If you are on the 70th percentile then seventy percent of your cultural-language group would score below you, and thirty percent would score the same or more. Mensans are, as I have said, on the 98th percentile, within the top two percent. Once you get the idea, you know what your score means with percentiles. With IQ you may not.

TAKING A PUZZLE SESSION

You may, of course, be one of those casual unmeticulous persons, like myself, who prefer making strict schedules for others rather than for yourself. You may prefer to wander idly through these puzzles, picking and trying one that takes your fancy here and there, like a maiden in the springtime wandering through the fields selecting a pretty leaf here, a flower there, and a curious stone yon. Or you might be a true puzzler, made of sterner stuff, one who is ready to confront the full rigour of my challenge.

To the former I say, "Blessings. Be off in your light hearted trivial way. I am not concerned with you. Be happy in your trivial light hearted way."

FOR THE SERIOUS PUZZLER

But to you, the latter, the men and women of hardihood and mental muscle, you the serious, the committed puzzle fighters, buckle on your brain armour and be ready. The war begins. For you I explain the system (unless you like to skip this and take it on as an extra puzzle).

First take the preliminary handicapping IQ test.

When you have your IQ result from chapter 2 you may start on chapter 3. It is best, but not necessary, to have a stop watch and note the time taken on each puzzle (or the start and finish time for each puzzle). You can even be so slack as to treat the session as a whole. If you do so, you must note the time of any interruptions. It is easy to take time off for a drink, a visit to the john (loo), or a phone call – and then cheat by continuing to think about the puzzle while you are not timed. How dishonest!

So for you others, the upright serious puzzlers, for each puzzle you note your start time or start your stop watch, then read the puzzle and note your answer and the time taken in the spaces provided. When you have finished and solved, or failed to solve, the fifteen puzzles in a chapter you may turn to the answer sheet at the end of it. The answers to the puzzles are given on a form where you may note your time in minutes (to the nearest half minute), the handicap time and if you solved it in less than the handicap time, your gain in points at 1 point per minute. There is no penalty where you exceed the handicap time on any question, and for each question correctly solved you add another 5 points at the bottom of the form. You carry forward your running total to the next chapter.

General Knowledge Quizzes

There are a number of general knowledge quizzes each with a number of questions. The allowance is one point for each question, and your added gain is the number you get right. There is no 5 point bonus in this case. Only if you answer them all correctly is there any gain from beating the time allowance.

The IQ Handicap

You can check up after a chapter or two, or at the end of the book. Take your running total, add two noughts and divide by your IQ. EG – score, 1000, IQ 150, therefore corrected score = 100,000/150 = 667.

For My American Readers

Some of the money puzzles are set in British pounds and pence. Older Americans may need to be reminded that there are now a mere 100 pence to the pound, not the confusing 240 that there used to be.

HOW TO GET SOME OF YOUR OWN BACK: PUZZLE DRIVES

Before you start your dreadful journey through the book I make a suggestion. The handicapping and marking scheme brings the possibility of a social opportunity for you to entrap other puzzle afficionados and fans to their doom. Instead of a bridge evening or a whist drive, you could invite your puzzler friends and rivals to a PUZZLE DRIVE. Mensans do it all the time. One chapter, photocopied – as many copies as contesting teams, supplies an evening's puzzling as you and your victims count your treasured total of puzzle points, an evening of gleeful pride and gloating triumph: or envy, hate and tension for you and those who have been, till then, your friends.

You can form small teams to compete frantically, or each person may struggle alone with his problems. You need a person appointed as timer, or a little programme on your PC with an alarm to give you a "start", "countdown" and "pencils down" for each puzzle. Each contestant or group gets a pile of pages with the backs up. The timer gives the time for the top puzzle and the top paper is turned. Then the timer counts down the minutes one by one – "20", "19", "18" and so on, as the contestants sweat and whisper. The contestants or teams write an answer when they are agreed, and hand it in to the timer, who marks the countdown time in minutes.

When time is up it is "pencils down". The timer gives the solution and those with a correct solution are credited with their gain, the countdown score when they declared the answer. The timer then starts the countdown for the next puzzle, and the contestants turn a new page and get going. Keep going until the session is over, then tot up scores and give a bow, a bag of gold, a bottle or a box to the winner(s).

ABOUT MENSA AND THE MENSA FOUNDATION

Puzzlers are often Mensans and vice versa. I am the Honorary International President of Mensa and the Chairman of the Mensa Foundation for Gifted Children.

MENSA (latin for table) is a round table society where no-one has precedence. It is a world-wide, non-profit society whose hundred odd thousand members have only one qualification. They have all achieved a score on a profession-ally supervised, standard test of general intelligence such that they are (roughly) in the top two percent of the general population. Children may be members of Mensa if they can be validly tested for IQ.

Founded in 1946 in Oxford, England, Mensa seeks to bring together a small sample of the intelligent people of the world for social and intellectual communion, friendship and mutual stimulus. It conducts social, psychological and opinion research but has no collective policies other than to foster intelligence for the general benefit. It has international, national and local organisations and its 103,000 members infest about 100 countries. British Mensa Ltd is the British branch. It has 40,000 members – 2,000 of them children. If you do well in my IQ test and the puzzles, you might like to send for a brochure and tests to Mensa Freepost, Wolverhampton in UK, to Mensa Brooklyn, New York in USA or International Mensa, 15 The Ivories, 6/8 Northampton Street, London N1 2HY, UK from other countries.

Mensa Foundation for Gifted Children

The Mensa Foundation for Gifted Children is a registered charity associated with and administered by British Mensa Ltd. It has been entrusted with the task of carrying out the Mensa aim of fostering intelligence for the benefit of humanity. It assists the parents of able children in the diagnosis of high intelligence by arranging intelligence and educational tests (free to those that cannot afford them) and by consultation, advice and action to obtain education for very promising children such that their potentiality shall be fulfilled for the advantage of the nations, the world and the children themselves. The Foundation also runs a quality assurance plan to certify suitable schools. UK readers can send applications for a brochure and IQ and EQ (Educational Quotient) tests to MENSA FREEPOST, WOLVERHAMPTON (envelope marked "CHILD").

Ready to start? Right! Here is your IQ test.

CHAPTER
TWO

THE SEREBRIAKOFF ADVANCED CULTURE-FAIR
IQ TEST

This test comes from my book "A Guide to Intelligence and Personality Testing". I am not claiming that it has been through all the rigorous research and validation testing to which clinical and professional tests are subjected. That sort of test is restricted to use by qualified psychometric psychologists and may not be published to the general public. This is a test made parallel to well established tests and validated on Mensa candidates who have been assessed on such tests. It gives a good first approximation guesstimate of where you stand. And, hee-hee! how much your handicap will be (as in golf) as you confront and tussle with the fiendish puzzles that are lined up to defeat you. The IQ tests are childishly simple at first, but – go on, be complacent, they get hellish as you struggle on. Tests have to be designed to stop everybody somewhere. There is no time limit.

Instructions

Try to work out the plan, or scheme, or order behind the way the central tiles are placed so as to find out which of the surrounding scattered tiles fits reasonably and logically into the space in the array.

Go through the 36 tests. There are eight 'tiles' in the central 3 x 3 array which have an inner bi-logical order. But one tile is missing. You will find it among the other ones which are scattered around. Find the missing tile among the lettered ones and write the letter above the tile against the question number on the answer page. Turn the book sideways so that you can see four puzzles each time you turn a page

9

THE ANSWER PAGE

Write the letter of the missing tile after each question number.

Question number	Answer letter	Question number	Answer letter
1	E	19	
2	C	20	G
3	E	21	G
4		22	H
5	B	23	D
6	B	24	G
7	H	25	A
8	J	26	A
9	K	27	
10	G	28	F
11	G	29	
12	B	30	A
13		31	E
14	H	32	I
15		33	C
16	C	34	E
17	H	35	
18	F	36	

Example

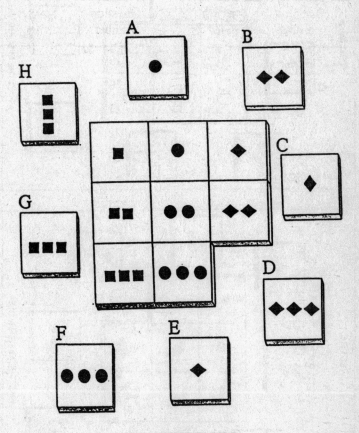

THE MISSING TILE IS D

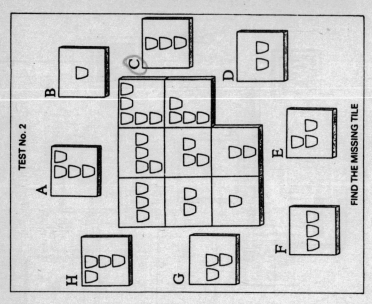

TEST No. 2

FIND THE MISSING TILE

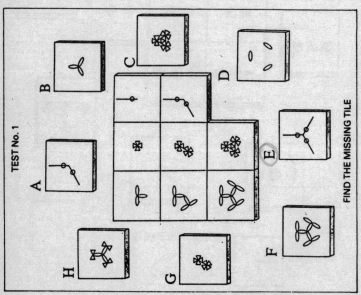

TEST No. 1

FIND THE MISSING TILE

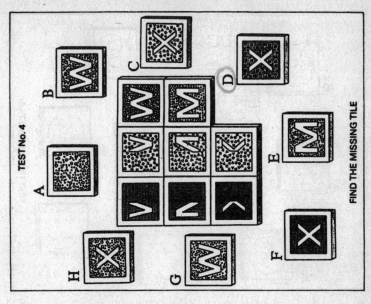

TEST No. 4

FIND THE MISSING TILE

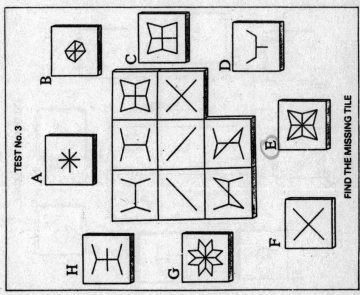

TEST No. 3

FIND THE MISSING TILE

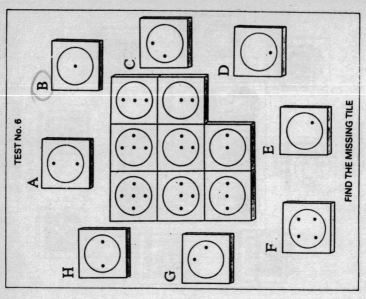

TEST No. 6

FIND THE MISSING TILE

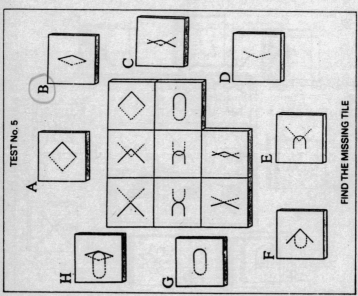

TEST No. 5

FIND THE MISSING TILE

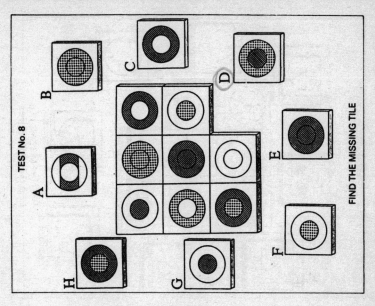

TEST No. 8

FIND THE MISSING TILE

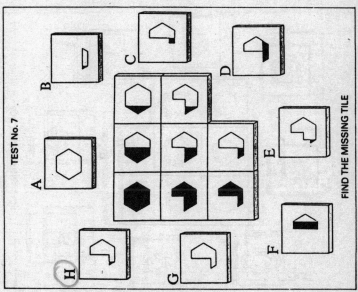

TEST No. 7

FIND THE MISSING TILE

15

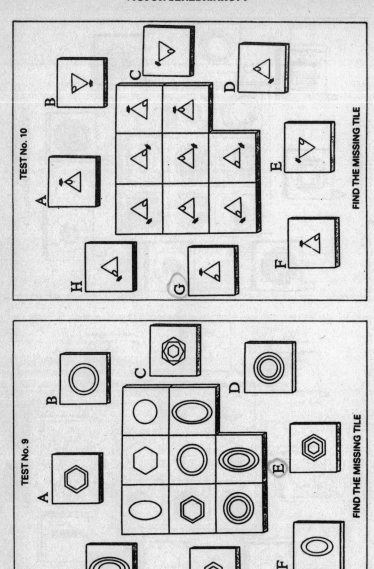

TEST No. 10

FIND THE MISSING TILE

TEST No. 9

FIND THE MISSING TILE

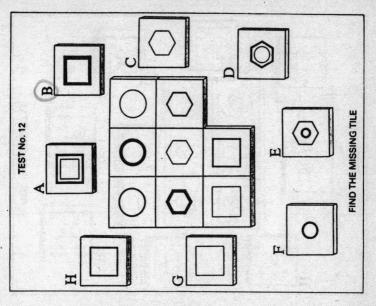

TEST No. 12

FIND THE MISSING TILE

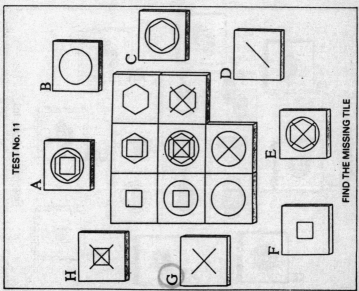

TEST No. 11

FIND THE MISSING TILE

17

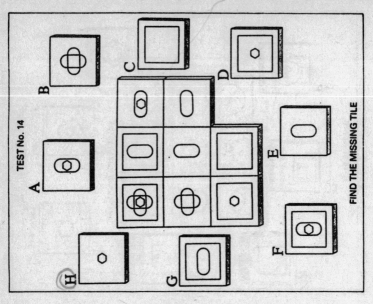

TEST No. 14

FIND THE MISSING TILE

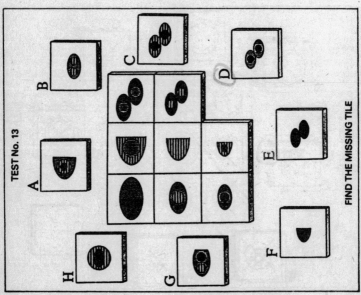

TEST No. 13

FIND THE MISSING TILE

18

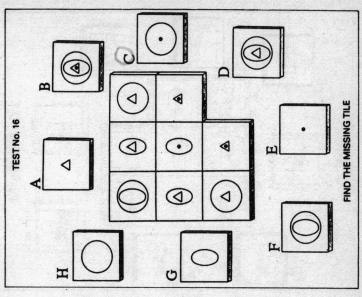

TEST No. 16

FIND THE MISSING TILE

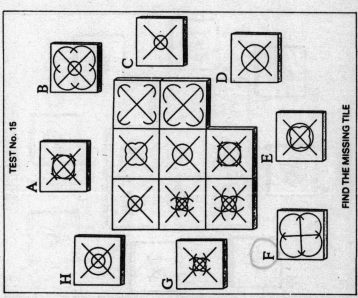

TEST No. 15

FIND THE MISSING TILE

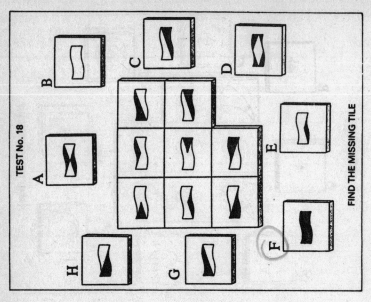

TEST No. 18

FIND THE MISSING TILE

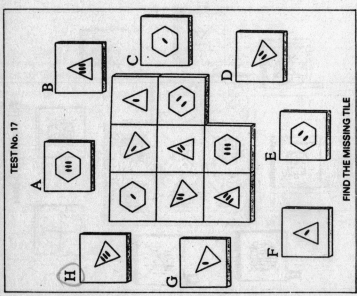

TEST No. 17

FIND THE MISSING TILE

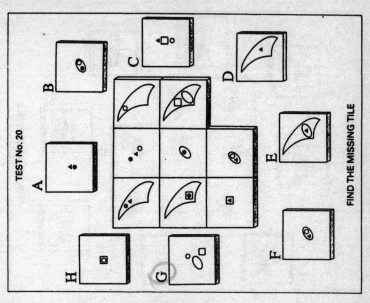

TEST No. 20

FIND THE MISSING TILE

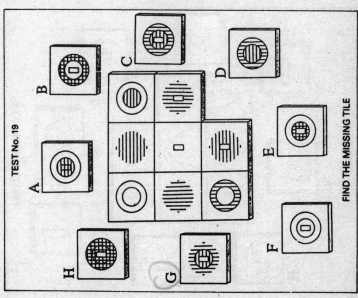

TEST No. 19

FIND THE MISSING TILE

21

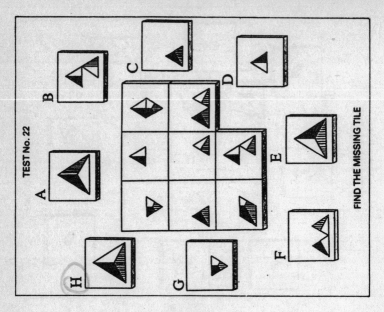

TEST No. 22

FIND THE MISSING TILE

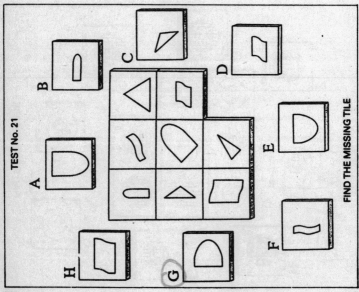

TEST No. 21

FIND THE MISSING TILE

GIPT—1

22

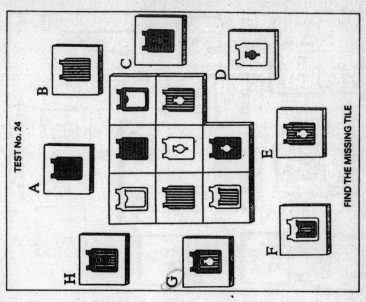

TEST No. 24

FIND THE MISSING TILE

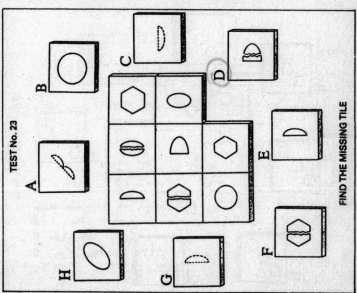

TEST No. 23

FIND THE MISSING TILE

23

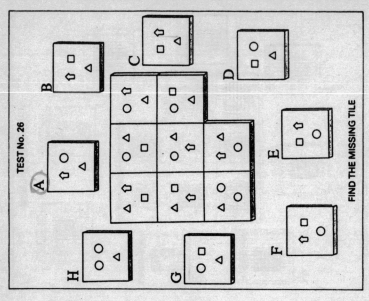

TEST No. 26

FIND THE MISSING TILE

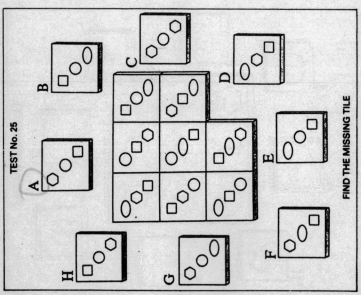

TEST No. 25

FIND THE MISSING TILE

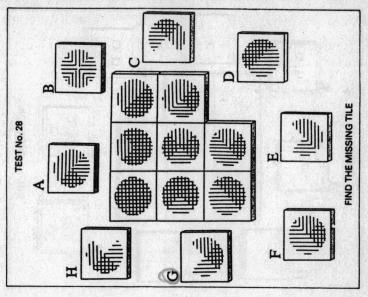

TEST No. 28

FIND THE MISSING TILE

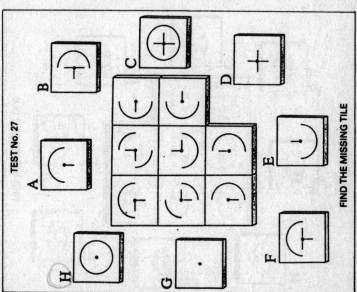

TEST No. 27

FIND THE MISSING TILE

25

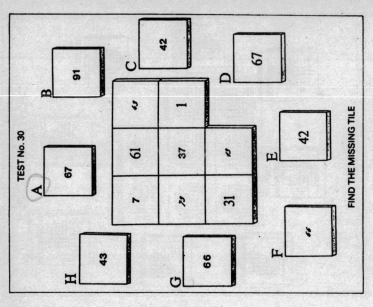

TEST No. 30

FIND THE MISSING TILE

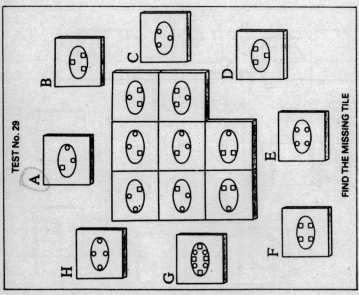

TEST No. 29

FIND THE MISSING TILE

26

TEST No. 32

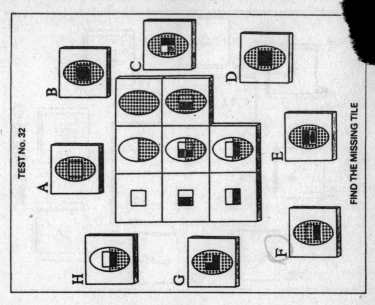

FIND THE MISSING TILE

TEST No. 31

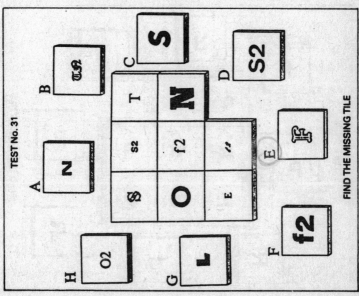

FIND THE MISSING TILE

TEST No. 34

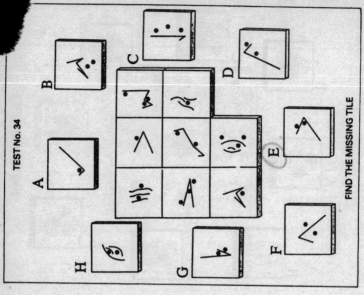

FIND THE MISSING TILE

TEST No. 33

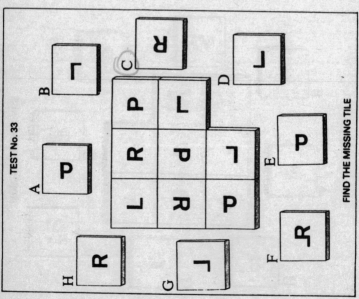

FIND THE MISSING TILE

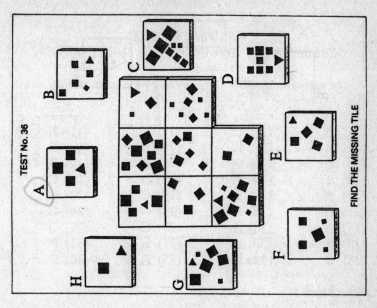

TEST No. 36

FIND THE MISSING TILE

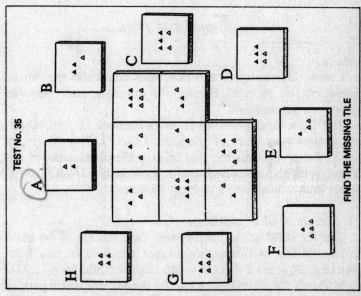

TEST No. 35

FIND THE MISSING TILE

29

ANSWERS TO THE
SEREBRIAKOFF ADVANCED CULTURE FAIR TEST

The question number is followed by the letter of the correct tile.

(1) E	(2) C	(3) E	(4) H
(5) B	(6) B	(7) H	(8) D
(9) E	(10) G	(11) G	(12) B
(13) E	(14) H	(15) D	(16) C
(17) H	(18) F	(19) C	(20) G
(21) G	(22) H	(23) D	(24) G
(25) A	(26) A	(27) G	(28) G
(29) F	(30) A	(31) E	(32) F
(33) C	(34) E	(35) E	(36) B

Total correct:

SCORING THE TEST

Adults
Check your answers and tick, then count the number of questions you got right. Be strict. If you made more than one guess you get no mark.

The Table which follows gives an estimate of your IQ rating against your score. If you score 18 (IQ 125) or more you are at the level at which preliminary Mensa candidates are asked to take a supervised test. A score above 25 (IQ 138) is better than that achieved by most Mensans.

Very bright or older children
Test the child as per instructions. Take the age of the child in months. Divide 180 by this number to make a decimal fraction (e.g. 12 years 2 months = 146 months. 180/146 = 1.233).

Multiply the child's IQ score on the test by this figure to obtain the child's adjusted IQ (e.g. a score of 6 on the test = IQ 101. 101 x 1.233 = adjusted IQ of 124.533 = 125).

SEREBRIAKOFF TEST SCORE TABLE

Score	IQ	Score	IQ
4	97	21	130
5	99	22	132
6	101	23	134
7	103	24	136
8	105	25	138
9	107	26	140
10	109	27	142
11	111	28	144
12	113	29	146
13	115	30	148
14	117	31	150
15	119	32	152
16	121	33	154
17	123	34	156
18	125	35	158
19	126	36	160
20	128		Mensa level

CHAPTER THREE

Target Time: 3 hours 37 minutes

THE CANNY TRICYCLIST

A poor but canny tricyclist goes for a 1000-mile tour. He has two spare tyres. He wants to use each tyre for the same distance and changes tyres to suit.

How many miles did each tyre travel?

ANSWER:

3.1	Minutes allowed	6
	Time taken	
	Points gained	

PIGGY BANK

You've had a tough time financially lately –
birthdays, wedding, whatall – and you are down
to your piggy bank collection. Using the broad
blade of a knife, you manage to get quite a few
coins out.

You find that you have £16, and you notice that
you have the same number of 10 pence, 20 pence
and 50 pence pieces. How many of each do you
have?

50×20=£10.
10+ 20=£2
20×20=£ 4.

ANSWER:

20

3.2	Minutes allowed	7
	Time taken	*1:25.*
	Points gained	

COUNT THOSE SPOONS!

Here is a special puzzle for Uri Spoonbender. This puzzle, however, is completely straight and there is only one exact answer. Can you tell us how many times you can form the word SPOON making sure that once you have used a combination of letters, you can't swap them round and count it twice. You can use each letter more than once, though – and watch out, this can be a bit tricky. Try and number the letters "S1, S2, P1, P2 etc."

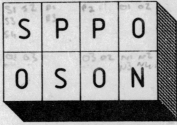

ANSWER:

24

3.3	Minutes allowed	9
	Time taken	
	Points gained	

COLLIDING ORBITS

a) Here is a planet orbiting its sun in a clockwise direction. An asteroid, however, is in a collision orbit with the planet. It travels in an anti-clockwise direction and is 60 degrees away from the intersection point of the orbits. The planet takes seven years to orbit the sun and the asteroid completes one orbit every 36 years.

How long will it be before they collide?

b) Why is the above question questionable?

ANSWER:

3.4	Minutes allowed	29
	Time taken	
	Points gained	

WHERE DO I LIVE?

Within this mass of letters there are seven four-lettered words. Work out what the words are and place them into the grid, in a special order, so that a town can be read downwards.

What is this town?

LNHAVAIESTRONE
PUIOANNEPKWTRS

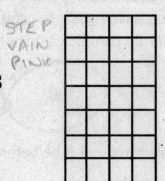

STEP
VAIN
PINK

ANSWER:

3.5	Minutes allowed	**20**
	Time taken	
	Points gained	

CLOCKS

"Little Sue", Big Ben's little sister, was correct at midnight but gains 51 minutes per hour.

You look at the clock and see that it shows 9.15 a.m. You know that the clock stopped exactly two hours ago.

What is the correct time now?

ANSWER:

	Minutes allowed	10
3.6	Time taken	
	Points gained	

HANDICAP

In a 150 yard race, Bobby beats Karen by 22 yards. The race is now run again with Bobby starting 26 yards behind the start line.

Assuming equal performance, who wins the race this time?

ANSWER:

3.7	Minutes allowed	7
	Time taken	
	Points gained	

COGGERY

Here are four cog wheels. The largest cog has 86 teeth, the next cog has 25 teeth, the next cog has 15 teeth and the smallest cog has 12 teeth. (The diagram below is only an example.)

How many revolutions will the largest cog make before all the cogs return to their original position?

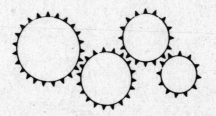

ANSWER:

3.8

Minutes allowed	15
Time taken	
Points gained	

A LEAKY TANKER

A petrol tanker travels at a speed of 42 mph. It is leaking petrol, however, and the petrol catches fire at the very moment it sets off. The petrol flame chases the tanker at a speed of 41½ mph.

If the tanker has stopped after 56¼ miles, when might it explode?

ANSWER:

3.9	Minutes allowed	8
	Time taken	
	Points gained	

FILL THE BLANKS

For this puzzle you must fill in the blanks so that each line of five numbers adds up to 125.

Can you tell us what number should replace the question mark?

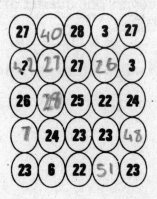

ANSWER:

42

3.10	Minutes allowed	6
	Time taken	
	Points gained	

WALK TIMES

A man goes on a sponsored walk. On the first day he covers one third of the total distance. On the second day he covers one half of the remaining distance. On the third day he covers one third of the remaining distance and on the fourth day he covers one quarter of the remaining distance.

He now has 25 miles left to go. How far has he travelled?

ANSWER:

3.11	Minutes allowed	15
	Time taken	
	Points gained	

TIME THE BOAT

A ship is battling against the stream to the safety of an island. It travels at a shuddering speed of 5 miles per hour, and is 15 miles away from safety. The flow of the water is 2^1/$_2$ miles per hour against the boat which uses 2^1/$_2$ gallons of fuel every hour and has a tank capacity of 15 gallons.

Will it reach safety, and if so how much fuel will it have left?

ANSWER:

<table>
<tr><td rowspan="3">**3.12**</td><td>Minutes allowed</td><td>**20**</td></tr>
<tr><td>Time taken</td><td></td></tr>
<tr><td>Points gained</td><td></td></tr>
</table>

TUNNELLING TRAIN

A train is travelling towards a tunnel at a speed of 30 mph. The tunnel is 6¹/₂ miles long and the train is ¹/₈ of a mile long.

How long will it take for the whole of the train to pass through the tunnel, from the moment the front of the train enters the tunnel to the moment the last of the rear of the train emerges from it?

ANSWER:

3.13

Minutes allowed	15
Time taken	
Points gained	

MARX AND WORK

The Marx brothers have taken on another job as furniture removal men and are loading tables onto a van. If Groucho was working on his own it would take him 12 minutes to fill an empty van and if Harpo was doing the same it would take him just 13$\frac{1}{2}$ minutes. However it would take Chico just 14 minutes to empty a full van. This of course is what is happening: Groucho and Harpo are loading the van whilst Chico is unloading the furniture and taking it back.

Can you tell us how long it would take for Groucho and Harpo to fill the van whilst Chico is unloading it at the same time?

ANSWER:

3.14	Minutes allowed	20
	Time taken	
	Points gained	

DIY CROSSWORD

The words down and across are given below, but you must decide where the blank squares are.

C	S	EAGERNESS
O	L	CATHARSIS
L	A	VIA AMUSE
L	C	LAMAS GNU
E	K	TAPE ROSE
A	N	TREK EASE
G	E	
U	S	S S
E	S	E T P A
		V U A R
		E N I E
		R G R A
		A S U T
		L T S A
		S E E M
		O M

3.15	Minutes allowed	30
	Time taken	
	Points gained	

ANSWERS

		FOR CORRECT ANSWERS		
		Your Time	Time Allowed	Points Gained
3.1	600 Miles		6	
3.2	20 of each coin		7	
3.3	Spoon can be formed 24 times		9	
3.4	a) A collision will occur after 42 years			
	b) Because the orbits are not astronomically possible		29	
3.5	Newport, Nail. Even. Wash Port. Open. Ruin. Task.		20	
3.6	The correct time is 7 am.		10	
3.7	Karen wins		7	
3.8	The largest cog will make 150 revolutions		15	
3.9	After 2 min 41 sec		8	
3.10	42		6	
3.11	125 miles		15	
3.12	The boat makes it with no fuel left		20	
3.13	13 min 15 sec		15	
3.14	11 min 38 sec		20	

POINTS CARRIED FORWARD

ANSWERS

POINTS BROUGHT FORWARD

3.15   Answer below   30

TOTAL POINTS GAINED

CHAPTER SUMMARY

Chapter Handicap Total:

Correct Answers x 5 points:

Chapter Total:

Brought Forward:

Running Total:

CHAPTER
FOUR

Target Time: 3 hours 12 minutes

YOU CUT AND I CHOOSE

The title gives a solution to fair shares for two when dividing cakes, but how can the principle be applied for three sharers?

Bill, Ben and Bertha share a cake. How do they arrange for the cutting to be fair?

ANSWER:

4.1	Minutes allowed	3
	Time taken	
	Points gained	

BREWMASTER

By starting at the centre square you can move in any direction except diagonally from square to touching square collecting the letters of the word BREW in any order. Can you tell us how many different ways there are of doing this?

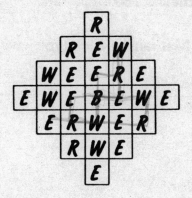

ANSWER:

4.2

Minutes allowed	6
Time taken	
Points gained	

EYING MARTIAN EYES

There are Martians with 4 eyes, Martians with 6 eyes, Martians with 8 eyes and Martians with 12 eyes. You know that there is an equal number of each type of Martian and you also know that the total number of eyes that the Martians have between them is 5,130.

How many Martians of each type have you got?

ANSWER:

4.3	Minutes allowed	**10**
	Time taken	
	Points gained	

MANAGING TIME

A company runs a Time Management course which it charges for. At the end of the first course the company's total takings were $3,895. There were more than 45 people on the course, but less than 100. Each person paid the same amount in full dollars only.

How many people went on the course and how much did the course cost?

ANSWER:

4.4

Minutes allowed	10
Time taken	
Points gained	

COSTING CASSETTES

A shop sells radios and cassette players. Cassette players cost 25 times as much as radios but of the ten items sold only one fifth were cassette players. Cassette players were sold at a price of £100 per 2.

How much did the shop earn from these sales?

ANSWER:

4.5

Minutes allowed	10
Time taken	
Points gained	

SYMBOLIC PROBLEM

Each different symbol has a different value. The numbers at the end of each row are the totals of the values of the symbols in that row. Can you work out the logic and fill in the missing value?

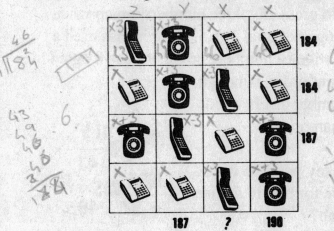

ANSWER:

4.6	Minutes allowed	8
	Time taken	
	Points gained	

BOMB CODE

A bomb has been planted on the Starship Enterprise. Mr Spock is desperately trying to defuse it by pressing numbers on a pad of buttons shown in our diagram. We know, though he doesn't, that he has to press any three numbers which when added together total 165.5. Once he has used a combination of numbers he cannot use it again in a different order, although each number can be used more than once.

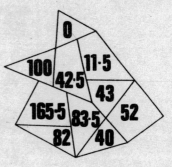

How many possible ways are there for him to defuse the bomb?

ANSWER:

4.7

Minutes allowed	15
Time taken	
Points gained	

ANAGRAMMAR

Each of the following words except one is an anagram of another word.

Which word has no English anagram?

SAILED   PRESENT   STERLING

REGINA   VIKING

ANSWER:

	Minutes allowed	15
4.8	Time taken	
	Points gained	

AGES AND AGES

Cressida didn't like to tell her age, but she didn't like to be rude either. So her mother usually answered for her. Her mother said, "I am just seven times as old as she is now. In 20 years, she will be just half the age that I will be then."

How old is little Cressida now?

3 - 21   4 = 28
23 - 40   2 L - 48

ANSWER:

4.9

	Minutes allowed	12
	Time taken	
	Points gained	

COSTING FRUIT

If an orange costs 18p, and a pineapple costs 27p, and a grape costs 15p – how much will a mango cost?

ANSWER:

4.10	Minutes allowed	5
	Time taken	
	Points gained	

PALINDROMING

A palindrome is a word, a phrase or a sentence that reads the same backwards as forwards. You will find two palindromic phrases defined below. Fill in the palindromes.

a) The zookeeper announces that he has captured two less than a dozen small beasts in a reticulated object.

b) Spoiled children of movie luminaries.

ANSWER:

4.11	Minutes allowed	30
	Time taken	
	Points gained	

BACKWARDS AND FORWARDS

Another palindrome puzzle. Can you find the
two palindromic phrases?

a) Query by rodent phobic person.

b) Comment by icecream and cake loving
overweight person.

ANSWER:

4.12	Minutes allowed	30
	Time taken	
	Points gained	

MEAT AND VEG

You've gone out shopping for groceries and meat. The joint costs twice as much as the vegetables, and the vegetables cost twice as much as the sweet. You spend the horrendous total of $14.

How much did the vegetables cost?

ANSWER:

4.13	Minutes allowed	3
	Time taken	
	Points gained	

MY FIRST – MY SECOND

By picking the right letter for each line, you can spell out a word of five letters. What is it?

My first is in FISH but not in SNAIL
My second is in RABBIT but not in KALE
My third is in UP but not in DOWN
My fourth is in TIARA but not in CROWN
My fifth is in TREE you'll plainly see,
The whole is a food for you and me.

ANSWER:

4.14

Minutes allowed	5
Time taken	
Points gained	

DIY CROSSWORD

The words down and across are given below, but you must decide where the blank squares are.

Grid	Words

SOT   TENET   E   L
DATA RUNE   X   I
MADAM VIE   T   V
NOMINATOR   R   E
I   A   Q   D   A   R
N   S   U   I   C   Y
N   S   E   M   T   M
     E   E   O   A
     T   N   R   N
  LIQUORICE
TOSS   E   B   O   O
EBON   N   E   N   M
       D   T   T   E
       S   A   O   N

Grid letters: Q, O, O, A

	Minutes allowed	30
4.15	Time taken	
	Points gained	

ANSWERS

		FOR CORRECT ANSWERS		
		Your Time	Time Allowed	Points Gained
4.1	One way is this: Bill cuts, Ben chooses, and they both trisect their pieces. Bertha chooses one piece from each		3	
4.2	7 ways		6	
4.3	171 Martians		10	
4.4	95 people each pay $41		10	
4.5	£116		10	
4.6	178		8	
4.7	There are 4 ways of scoring 165.5		15	
4.8	Viking has no anagram		15	
4.9	Her mother is 28 and Cressida is 4		12	
4.10	15p – 3p per letter		5	
4.11	a) Ten animals I slam in a net b) Star brats		30	
4.12	a) Was it a rat I saw b) Desserts I stressed		30	
4.13	$4		3	
4.14	Fruit		5	

POINTS CARRIED FORWARD

ANSWERS

	FOR CORRECT ANSWERS		
	Your Time	Time Allowed	Points Gained

POINTS BROUGHT FORWARD

4.15   Answer below | 30

TOTAL POINTS GAINED

CHAPTER SUMMARY

Chapter Handicap Total:

Correct Answers x 5 points:

Chapter Total:

   Brought Forward:

   Running Total:

CHAPTER FIVE

Target Time: 3 hours 32 minutes

BOUNCING CHEQUE LOSS

You are a second-hand furniture dealer. Your first customer of the day buys a settee for $25 and pays with a cheque, changes his mind and asks for a $15 chair instead. With an empty till, you cash the cheque with a neighbour and give the buyer a $10 note as change.

The cheque bounces and you have to borrow $25 to pay the neighbour. The chair cost you $11. How much money have you lost?

ANSWER:

5.1	Minutes allowed	5
	Time taken	
	Points gained	

SECRET SENTENCE

There is a sentence hidden in this square. You have to find the start letter and unravel the sentence. All the letters are used and you can move in any direction to any touching square, and by touching we even mean if it is only the corners that are touching.

D	E	D	N	E	L	E
N	I	O	N	E	P	H
T	M	A	T	N	A	V
N	E	I	I	N	E	E
S	S	T	S	F	R	R
B	A	S	N	S	O	G
N	A	E	L	U	T	E

ANSWER:

5.2

Minutes allowed	20
Time taken	
Points gained	

CUBISM

Here is the spread-out pattern of a box. When it is folded it will make a cube. You must decide which of the completed cubes below cannot be made from this.

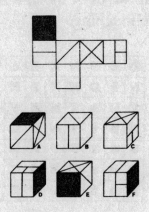

ANSWER:

5.3

Minutes allowed	10
Time taken	
Points gained	

DEPRIVED PROVERB 1

The following proverb has had all of the vowels taken out, and the remaining letters broken up into groups of four letters each. Replace the vowels and find the proverb.

BRDS FFTH RFLC KTGT HR

ANSWER:

5.4

Minutes allowed	3
Time taken	
Points gained	

DEPRIVED PROVERB 2

Here is another popular proverb, treated in the
same way as the previous puzzle.

Can you decipher it?

FLND   HSMN   YRSN   PRTD

ANSWER:

5.5	Minutes allowed	**5**
	Time taken	
	Points gained	

MUFFIN RACE

At a mass muffin eating contest Elizabeth eats an average of 22 muffins in her first 10 sittings. After a further 20 sittings her average increases to 34 muffins.

Can you tell us what her average was for her last 20 sittings only?

ANSWER:

5.6

Minutes allowed	10
Time taken	
Points gained	

MURPHY

The following coiled sentence in the box will rhyme with the first line. It is a saying that will complete the poem (or couplet, if you prefer).

MURPHY'S LAW IS VERY FINE

```
T  K  K  O  E
I  E  C  F  N
P  E  E  F  I
S  Y  N  T  L
O  U  R  H  E
```

ANSWER:

	Minutes allowed	15
5.7	Time taken	
	Points gained	

WINGLES, WONKLES

If 6 wingles and 3 wonkles cost 15¢, and you can buy 9 wonkles and 3 wingles for the same 15¢, how much will it cost you to buy 100 wonkles?

ANSWER:

5.8	Minutes allowed	6
	Time taken	
	Points gained	

THE 'I's HAVE IT!

All answers begin with the letter I.

Answers

1. Little devil
2. Sub continent
3. Kind of architecture
4. Creeper
5. Mrs Ghandi
6. Mesembryanthemum
7. Cretan mountain
8. Large lizard
9. Measuring worm
10. Austrian city at foot of Brenner pass
11. Metal era
12. German medal
13. Home of Baghdad
14. Son of Abraham and Hagar
15. Elephant tusk

5.9	Minutes allowed	18
	Time taken	
	Points gained	

TIMED CROSSWORD

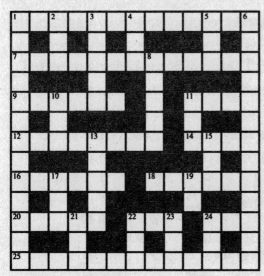

Across

1. Avocado (9,4)
7. Kentish coastal bogs (6,7)
9. Cell fats (6)
11. Legionnaire's hat (4)
12. Vision adjuster (8)
14. Head of Faculty (4)
16. Paired with Hardy (6)
18. Arch of the foot (6)
20. Giver (5)
22. Large cup (3)
24. & 24 down A dance (3-3)
25. Colourful poison (6,7)

Down

1. Funny Spring day (5,5,4)
2. Astronomical abbreviation (3)
3. Excessive desire (5)
4. Kind of beret? (3)
5. Runic letter (3)
6. A scared red's reaction perhaps (8,5)
8. Scottish isle (5)
10. Container (3)
11. Young goat (3)
13. Loud yell of acclamation (5)
15. Newt (3)
17. Another container (3)
19. Type of nurse (abbrev) (2)
21. Was friendly with pussy cat (3)
22. Extinct bird (3)
23. Neon, for example (3)
24. See 24 across (3)

5.10	Minutes allowed	45
	Time taken	
	Points gained	

SAME, BUT DIFFERENT

Look at the sixteen rectangles in this diagram. In each one there is a series of objects arranged in a different order. There are some objects repeated more than once in some squares. Can you tell which pairs of squares can be considered identical, since they contain exactly the same objects, although maybe not in the same order.

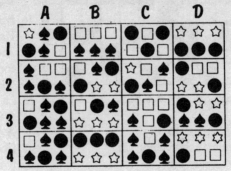

ANSWER:

5.11	Minutes allowed	15
	Time taken	
	Points gained	

COME FOLLOW, FOLLOW!

You wish to get from A to Z and must follow the arrows. How many different ways can you find to accomplish this task?

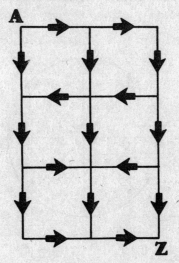

ANSWER:

5.12

Minutes allowed	10
Time taken	
Points gained	

WHAT LOGIC?

Can you work out the logic behind this series of numbers and replace the two exclamation marks with the correct positive numbers?

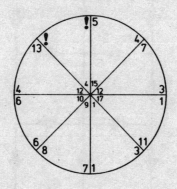

ANSWER:

5.13

Minutes allowed	10
Time taken	
Points gained	

EGGS

A farmer sells brown eggs and white eggs.
Brown eggs are sold for £6 for ten and cost three
times as much as the white eggs. The farmer
sells 150 eggs of which one eighth are brown.
Perhaps you can now see what we mean by
'good in parts': he must have been a good
salesman to sell three quarters of an egg!

Ignore this obvious error. How much money
should he make by selling the eggs?

ANSWER:

5.14

Minutes allowed	10
Time taken	
Points gained	

DIY CROSSWORD

The words down and across are given below, but you must decide where the blank squares are.

O								
	O							
							R	Y
	S		P					
							R	
M								S

SUPPORT   HAS   P
ARK   ATTAR   R
METE   ONYX   E
   U   U   P   P
   P   O   R   A
   S   T   N   R
   E   T   E
   T   R
APES   EWE   TRY
EAT   REBUS   HAS
O   T   A   Y   B   E   S   A   ROE
R   H   W   E   A   A   T   S   URNS
A   E   E   T   R   R   Y   K
L   M   S   S

5.15	Minutes allowed	30
	Time taken	
	Points gained	

ANSWERS

		FOR CORRECT ANSWERS	
	Your Time	Time Allowed	Points Gained
5.1	You lost what the thief gained , i.e. $10 + a chair = $21. Loss of profit is not loss of money.	5	
5.2	An elephant never forgets unless it is an absent-minded one	20	
5.3	F	10	
5.4	Birds of a feather flock together	3	
5.5	A fool and his money are soon parted	5	
5.6	40 muffins	10	
5.7	It keeps your neck off the line (start second letter down, left hand side)	15	
5.8	$1 (wonkles are 1¢, and wingles 2¢)	6	
5.9	Imp, India, Ionic, Ivy, Indira, Ice plant, Ida, Iguana, Inch worm, Innsbruck, Iron Age, Iron Cross, Iraq, Ishmael, Ivory	18	

CARRIED FORWARD

ANSWERS

	FOR CORRECT ANSWERS		
	Your Time	Time Allowed	Points Gained

BROUGHT FORWARD

		Time Allowed
5.10	**Across. 1.** Alligator Pear **7.** Romney marshes **9.** Lipids **11.** Kepi **12.** Optician **14.** Dean **16.** Laurel **18.** Instep **20.** Donor **22.** Mug **24 & 24 Down** Can-can **25.** Yellow Arsenic **Down. 1.** April Fool's Day **2.** L.E.M. **3.** Greed **4.** Tam **5.** Edh **6.** Russians Panic **8.** Arran **10.** Pot **11.** Kid **13.** Cheer **15.** Eft **17.** Urn **19.** S.R. **21.** Owl **22.** Moa **23.** Gas **24.** See 24 Across	45
5.11	D1 & B4, A3 and A4	15
5.12	10 ways	10
5.13	0 and 1 (numbers at circumference of segment added together equal number at centre of opposite segment)	10
5.14	£37.50	10

CARRIED FORWARD

ANSWERS

		FOR CORRECT ANSWERS	
	Your Time	Time Allowed	Points Gained

POINTS BROUGHT FORWARD

5.15 Answer below | | 30 |

TOTAL POINTS GAINED

CHAPTER SUMMARY

Chapter Handicap Total:

Correct Answers x 5 points:

Chapter Total:

Brought Forward:

Running Total:

CHAPTER
SIX

Target Time: 3 hours 4 minutes

SCREWY ENIGMA

You have two screws as in the illustration. The distance between the two heads is 85.72mm. The pitch is 2.715mm. You hold the two screws together as shown and, without allowing them to rotate, you move the right hand screw around the left hand screw, as shown in the illustration, keeping them engaged together. You rotate this three times exactly. What is now the distance between the heads of the screws?

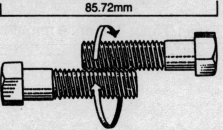

85.72mm

ANSWER:

6.1	Minutes allowed	5
	Time taken	
	Points gained	

LETTER BALANCE

The top and bottom sets of scales in this diagram balance perfectly. How many of the missing letters are needed to balance the middle set?

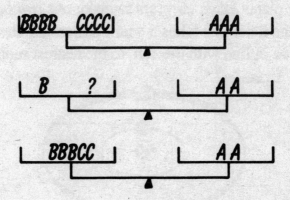

ANSWER:

6.2	Minutes allowed	15
	Time taken	
	Points gained	

TIMING ORBITS

This is a planetary system of two planets orbiting their sun. The sun is smaller than the planets because it is going out. The planets are in line with the sun and are about to rotate around it. The outer planet takes 15 years to make one revolution and the inner one takes 5 years. When will they next be in line with the sun, to the nearest month?

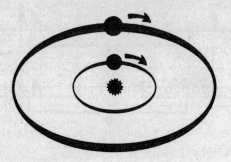

ANSWER:

6.3	Minutes allowed	15
	Time taken	
	Points gained	

TIMED CROSSWORD

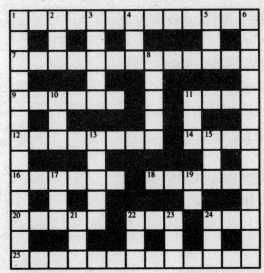

Across

1. One of the Beatles (4,9)
7. North . . . (4,5,4,)
9. A line for reefing (6)
11. Husks of cereal grain (4)
12. Cloudy (8)
14. John McEnroe perhaps (4)
16. Christian festival (6)
18. Relaxed position (2,4)
20. Hollow muscular organ (5)
22. Mineral spring (30)
24. Donkey (3)
25. Early Christian (5,8)
15. & 21. Submerged valley (3)
17. & 22D. Navigational abbreviation (1,1,1)
19. Exclamation of surprise (2)
23. Type of tree (3)
24. Everything (3)

Down

1. Fathom (5,8)
2. The 'Enterprise' perhaps (1,1,1)
3. Stone builder (5)
4. Computer abbreviation (1,1,1)
5. Scottish 'no' (3)
6. A busy postman's reaction perhaps (3,7,3)
8. Or trick perhaps (5)
10. Kind of deer (3)
11. Monkhouse, Hope, etc (3)
13. Swindle (5)

6.4	Minutes allowed	45
	Time taken	
	Points gained	

DO YOU KNOW?

All answers begin with the letter J.

Answers

1. Another name for a hyacinth
2. Variety of orange
3. Semi precious stone or colour
4. Unidentified murderer from around 1888
5. A short leather strap in falconry
6. An island in Indonesia
7. Pier or dock
8. Old rustic dance
9. Another name for Jupiter
10. A judo expert
11. Seventh month
12. A member of a jury
13. A Chinese sailing vessel
14. Sweater or pullover
15. River in N. E. Africa

6.5	Minutes allowed	15
	Time taken	
	Points gained	

VASE TRADING

Bill bought an antique vase last year and sold it for 10% more than it cost. Jim bought an antique lamp, couldn't get rid of it, and sold it for 10% less than he paid. Then, just to compound the problem, Bill bought another vase at exactly the same price as the first, couldn't get rid of it, and took a 10% cut; and Jim bought an identical lamp and sold it for 10% more than he paid, which was the same price he paid for the first one.

Which of the two men made money or lost money on that series of deals?

ANSWER:

6.6	Minutes allowed	10
	Time taken	
	Points gained	

BEAN GUESSES

Mary's corner shop was losing some business to the new supermarket, so she ran one of those 'Guess the jelly beans in the jar' competitions. It was a very small jar indeed. Ann guessed 43 beans, Bet guessed 34 beans, Charles guessed 41 beans. One of them was off by 6 beans, another by 3 beans and another by only 1.

How many beans were there really?

ANSWER:

6.7	Minutes allowed	5
	Time taken	
	Points gained	

COMMITTEE HATER

The following cynical comment has had all the vowels removed, and the remaining letters broken up into groups of four. Replace the vowels and solve the comment.

CMMT   TSGR   PTHT   KPSM   NTSB
TWST   SHRS

ANSWER:

	Minutes allowed	10
6.8	Time taken	
	Points gained	

NUMBER WISE?

Take the number of states in the United States, multiply by the number of lives a cat is supposed to have, divide by the Roman numeral X, and subtract the number of cents in a U.S. quarter.

What is left?

ANSWER:

6.9	Minutes allowed	3
	Time taken	
	Points gained	

SELECT THEM SOCKS

You have brown, blue, black and green socks in your drawer, in the ratio of 2 to 3, to 4, to 5 pairs. How many socks must you take out to be sure of having a pair?

ANSWER:

6.10

Minutes allowed	3
Time taken	
Points gained	

FOUR LETTER WORDS

What is the 4-letter word which when placed in front of the following four words will make each of them into a new word?

LINE   BOAT   LIKE   STYLE

ANSWER:

6.11	Minutes allowed	3
	Time taken	
	Points gained	

A DISTRAUGHT LAD

What 4 letters can be re-arranged to make sense
– and two different words – in the following
sentence:

The little boy was absolutely distraught: "That
wicked hunter set a . . . . and caught my pet; I
cannot bear to . . . . with him, but I don't know
what to do."

ANSWER:

6.12	Minutes allowed	3
	Time taken	
	Points gained	

WAYS WITH GUY

"This Guy was hot stuff!" In this diagram you will find the letters of the name "Guy". Can you tell us how many ways there are of forming this name? You are permitted to use each letter more than once, but the same combination of letters cannot be used again in a different order.

ANSWER:

6.13

Minutes allowed	12
Time taken	
Points gained	

EVERY LEAF IS COUNTED

Can you count the leaves? How many ways are there of tracing the word 'leaf', starting each time from the centre circle. You can only move to touching circles.

ANSWER:

6.14	Minutes allowed	10
	Time taken	
	Points gained	

DIY CROSSWORD

The words down and across are given below, but you must decide where the blank squares are.

			N					
K								
		F						
			Y					
				Z				
								D

ELEVENSES P U
UPON KIN R N
RUE APSE E F
INFORMERS C E
STY TAR U T
STUN ORE R T
JUG BRED S E
O E C L O R
U R R A R S
R E Y P

B S U N T F
E K S E I E
T I E S N Z
A P D T

6.15	Minutes allowed	30
	Time taken	
	Points gained	

ANSWERS

		FOR CORRECT ANSWERS	
	Your Time	Time Allowed	Points Gained
6.1	85.72mm. The distance will not change.	5	
6.2	6 Cs	15	
6.3	3 years and 9 months	15	
6.4	**Across 1.** Paul McCartney **7.** East, South West **9.** Earing **11.** Bran **12.** Overcast **14.** Brat **16.** Easter **18.** At ease **20.** Heart **22.** Spa **24.** Ass **25.** Roman Catholic **Down 1.** Piece together **2.** U.S.S. **3.** Mason **4.** C.P.U. **5.** Nae **6.** Yet another sac **8.** Treat **10.** Roe **11.** Bob **13.** Cheat **15.** Ria **17.** S.H.A. **19.** Eh **21.** Ria **22.** S.H.A. **23.** Ash **24.** All	45	
6.5	Jacinth. Jaffa. Jade. Jack the Ripper. Jess. Java. Jetty. Jig. Jove. Judoka. July. Juror. Junk. Jumper. Juba	15	
6.6	Each of them wound up with 99% ($^{11}/_{10}$ x $^9/_{10}$) of their original investment	10	

CARRIED FORWARD

ANSWERS

		Your Time	Time Allowed	Points Gained
	BROUGHT FORWARD			
6.7	40 Beans		5	
6.8	A committee is a group that keeps minutes but wastes hours		10	
6.9	20 (= 50 x 9 ÷ 10 - 25)		3	
6.10	One more than the number of colours – 5 (all the rest has nothing to do with it)		3	
6.11	Life		3	
6.12	APRT (trap, part)		3	
6.13	The word GUY can be made 24 times		12	
6.14	There are only 4 ways of making the word LEAF		10	
6.15	See overleaf			
	CARRIED FORWARD			

ANSWERS

	FOR CORRECT ANSWERS		
	Your Time	Time Allowed	Points Gained
POINTS BROUGHT FORWARD			
6.15 Answer below		30	
TOTAL POINTS GAINED			

CHAPTER SUMMARY

Chapter Handicap Total:

Correct Answers x 5 points:

Chapter Total:

Brought Forward:

Running Total:

CHAPTER SEVEN

Target Time: 3 hours 57 minutes

ENCOMPASSING AN OVAL

A pair of compasses draws a circle. How, without changing the radius, can you make it draw an oval? You have to fix a radius, then make one rotation from a fixed point to draw an oval where the curvature changes continuously all the way around the perimeter and the pencil produces a doubly symmetrical figure where one axis is more than the unaltered radius.

How can it be done?

ANSWER:

7.1	Minutes allowed	20
	Time taken	
	Points gained	

SQUARE UP TO THIS

Can you complete this number square so that each row and each column of five numbers adds up to 220?

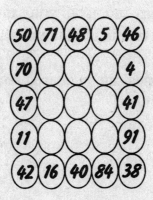

ANSWER:

7.2	Minutes allowed	30
	Time taken	
	Points gained	

FIREWORKS WORKOUT

Now it's time to count fireworks. Starting from the bottom left hand corner and working your way up to the top right hand corner, you must collect the letters of the word 'Fireworks'. You can collect the letters in any order, but you can only move from segment to touching segment.

How many times can you make the word 'Fireworks'?

ANSWER:

7.3	Minutes allowed	15
	Time taken	
	Points gained	

ORBITAL LINE-UP

Two satellites leave the earth's atmosphere and begin to orbit the earth. They start in line with each other and both orbit in a clockwise direction. The inner satellite makes one revolution every three years, and the outer satellite makes one revolution every nine years. Can you tell us when they will next form a straight line with themselves and the earth.

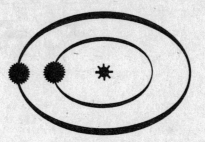

ANSWER:

7.4	Minutes allowed	15
	Time taken	
	Points gained	

UNMAKEABLE BOXES

Four of the boxes below are made up versions of the plan view, and two are not. Can you tell which two boxes these are?

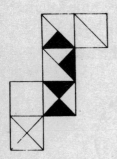
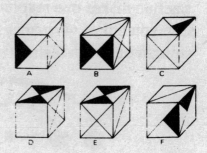

ANSWER:

7.5	Minutes allowed	10
	Time taken	
	Points gained	

CREEPY CRAWLERS

Imagine you are a caterpillar and are crawling down the veins of an enormous leaf, like the one shown below. Unfortunately, a fellow caterpillar has chewed its way through the main part of the leaf, so to get from one end of the leaf to the other you have to crawl along the lines following the arrows shown.

How many different ways are there of doing this?

ANSWER:

7.6	Minutes allowed	5
	Time taken	
	Points gained	

BLACK HOLE

A planet revolves around a sun in a clockwise direction and makes one revolution every 42 years. An asteroid, which revolves around a black hole in an anti-clockwise direction, is 40° away from where both orbits intersect. The asteroid makes an orbit every 27 years. Can you tell when they will collide?

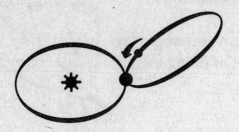

ANSWER:

7.7	Minutes allowed	20
	Time taken	
	Points gained	

PINBALL PINDOWN

Look at this strange pinball table. Imagine your ball is fired from any outside corner, and is allowed to hit four bumpers. You must remember that a ball that is fired from a corner cannot then hit another outside corner, and can only hit four numbers, excluding the corner. What is the highest possible score, and how many ways are there of achieving it?

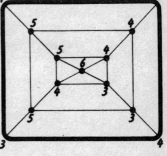

ANSWER:

7.8	Minutes allowed	**15**
	Time taken	
	Points gained	

ODD SIGNS

This strange signpost may not appear to contain any logic, but actually it does. Each letter is given a value and the total values of the letters in each town is its corresponding distance.

Can you work out the logic and tell us the distance to Paris?

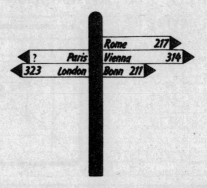

ANSWER:

7.9	Minutes allowed	30
	Time taken	
	Points gained	

BIRD WATCHING

Which twenty birds can be found in this diagram? Each of the names can be read forwards or backwards in a straight line, vertically, horizontally or diagonally.

O	S	P	R	E	Y	Y	A	J	P
Q	P	A	C	D	E	R	S	K	W
T	E	R	N	K	H	C	N	I	F
A	R	P	R	O	B	I	N	T	L
K	B	U	Z	Z	A	R	D	E	T
C	T	F	A	N	S	L	R	O	O
O	D	F	L	W	D	T	T	W	R
C	U	I	A	K	S	O	L	R	R
E	C	N	R	E	M	U	V	X	A
R	K	S	K	C	O	C	A	E	P

ANSWER:

7.10	Minutes allowed	12
	Time taken	
	Points gained	

HIDDEN QUOTATION

This box of letters is more than just a box of letters! By starting at one of the letters you can trace a hidden quotation by going from one letter to another. You can move from a square to any touching square, vertically, horizontally or diagonally, and must use every letter.

O	E	K	O	W
M	C	G	N	L
S	E	D	E	L
W	B	U	M	I
I	T	O	E	N
S	D	S	R	G

ANSWER:

7.11

Minutes allowed	10
Time taken	
Points gained	

AND ANOTHER

Now try this hidden quotation. The instructions are exactly the same as for the previous puzzle. What is the quotation this time?

P	L	A	U	T
W	I	N	U	A
O	E	L	N	M
Y	L	G	N	O
T	E	O	N	D
H	R	E	I	D

ANSWER:

7.12

Minutes allowed	10
Time taken	
Points gained	

MEAN SPEED

A competitor in this year's car rally completes a stage at an average speed of 26 miles per hour. At the next stage his average speed greatly improves. In fact, it is three times faster than before, i.e. 78 miles per hour. Both stages were exactly the same length.

Can you tell us his average speed for both stages?

ANSWER:

7.13	Minutes allowed	10
	Time taken	
	Points gained	

SLOPPY CASHIER

You enter your local bank to cash a cheque. As usual there is a long queue, and only one out of five cashiers is serving. By the time you get to the cashier you're fed up with waiting and he is in a total mess. In fact he is in such a state that he gives you pounds for pence shown on the cheque and pence for pounds. Noticing this, you quickly rush off and spend 23 pence. Counting your cash you find that you have exactly twice the amount of your original cheque.

Can you tell us how much the cheque was for?

ANSWER:

7.14

Minutes allowed	5
Time taken	
Points gained	

DIY CROSSWORD

The words down and across are given below, but you must decide where the blank squares are.

I								S
							O	
			Q					
O								D

ELUDE NOT A
ICE KEEPS S
REQUIEM SIR S
WEED IRIS C U
OPAL CATS A P R
RAM NOR P E
ORE A E D
A N E
I D O E R
R I D E M O E
E E E A E

I S H T T U E E E A E
N T E I O S
K E R R R U
Y P D O E

Minutes allowed	30
7.15 Time taken	
Points gained	

ANSWERS

7.1 Wrap the paper around a bottle or rolling pin (see illustration). Then draw a circle, and when the paper is unwrapped the oval will be seen.

Bottle

Pair of Compasses

Paper

20

7.2 One answer is:
50 71 48   5 46
70 46 50 50   4
47 49 44 39 41
11 38 38 42 91
42 16 40 84 38

30

7.3 25 times

15

7.4 After 27 months

15

7.5 C and D can't be made

10

CARRIED FORWARD

125

ANSWERS

| | | FOR CORRECT ANSWERS | | |
		Your Time	Time Allowed	Points Gained
	BROUGHT FORWARD			
7.6	11 ways		5	
7.7	After 84 years		20	
7.8	The highest possible score is 25, which can only be achieved one way		15	
7.9	The distance to Paris is 270½ miles. A = 42½, B = 43½ , etc		30	
7.10	Turkey. Buzzard. Puffin. Peacock. Kestrel. Parrot. Cockatoo. Owl. Dove. Emu. Swan. Osprey. Tern. Redcap. Jay. Lark. Robin. Kite. Finch. Duck		12	
7.11	The quotation is "Knowledge comes but wisdom lingers"		10	
7.12	The quotation is "Autumn nodding o'er the yellow plain"		10	
7.13	Average speed for both stages = 39 m.p.h.		10	
7.14	The cheque was for £25.51		5	
	CARRIED FORWARD			

ANSWERS

FOR CORRECT ANSWERS

| | Your Time | Time Allowed | Points Gained |

POINTS BROUGHT FORWARD

7.15 Answer below

30

TOTAL POINTS GAINED

```
I R I S   C A T S
N O R   A   N O T
K E E P S   O R E
Y     S   D   P
  R E Q U I E M
T   N   R       H
I C E   E L U D E
R A M   D   S I R
O P A L   W E E D
```

CHAPTER SUMMARY

Chapter Handicap Total:

Correct Answers x 5 points:

Chapter Total:

Brought Forward:

Running Total:

CHAPTER EIGHT

Target Time: 3 hours 16 minutes

MONUMENTAL PROBLEM

A 10-tonne statue with a flat bottom has to be settled by crane upon a larger pedestal. There is no way of lifting the statue except by slings under the base.

How do you arrange to set the statue on the pedestal and then get the slings out?

ANSWER:

8.1	Minutes allowed	10
	Time taken	
	Points gained	

WHAT'S A SYMBOL WORTH?

Each different symbol has a different value, and the numbers are the totals of the symbols in that row or column.

Can you tell us the total of the top row?

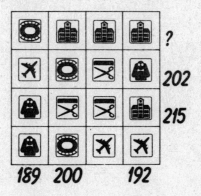

ANSWER:

8.2	Minutes allowed	5
	Time taken	
	Points gained	

HOW MANY ANAGRAMS?

How many anagrams can you find of the following word?

TREAD

ANSWER:

8.3

Minutes allowed	**5**
Time taken	
Points gained	

GET IN GEAR

Four cogs are in constant mesh as the example shows. The largest cog has 18 teeth, the next cog has 17 teeth, the next 16 teeth and the smallest has 15 teeth.

How many revolutions must the first cog make before all the cogs return to their original position?

ANSWER:

8.4	Minutes allowed	**15**
	Time taken	
	Points gained	

WEIGH IN WITH THIS

Can you tell how many symbols are missing from the bottom right hand balance?

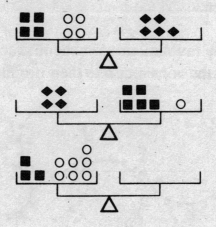

ANSWER:

	Minutes allowed	10
8.5	Time taken	
	Points gained	

BID FOR ART

At an art auction each painting cost the same price and each customer only bought one painting. There were more than 3 buyers but less than 100, and the auctioneers took £1698.

Can you tell us how many customers there were and the price of each painting?

ANSWER:

8.6

Minutes allowed	15
Time taken	
Points gained	

SOCCER GOALS

In the last soccer season Adam scored 34 more goals than Brian, who scored 26 less than Chris. We also know that Ed scored 8 more than Dave, Chris scored 13 more than Ed and the total number of goals scored by Brian and Ed was 37.

How many goals were scored altogether by the five players?

ANSWER:

8.7	Minutes allowed	10
	Time taken	
	Points gained	

BOOZE COST

A wine seller earned £532 in a day. Red wine costs three times as much as white wine. Of the 140 bottles sold, only one quarter were red.

How much would 5 bottles of red wine cost?

ANSWER:

8.8

Minutes allowed	8
Time taken	
Points gained	

TIMED CROSSWORD

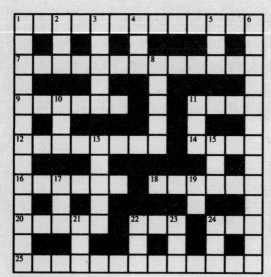

Across

1. Paul Daniels maybe? (7,6)
7. Musical instruments (6,7)
9. Seasides (6)
11. Clarified butter (4)
12. Cumbrian beauty spot (6)
14. Result of one of Quasimodo's duties (4)
16. Loyalty (6)
18. Obscure Indian river (6)
20. Architectural form (6)
22. Male of **4D** (3)
24. Teutonic state (abbrev.) (3)
25. Arithmetical term (6,7)

Down

1. Party game (7,6)
2. Narrow inlet (3)
3. Escape by luck
4. Anagrammed sheep (3)
5. Obsolete violin
6. Mountain range of Europe (13)
8. Moist atmosphere (5)
10. The first man of Norse mythology (3)
11. Primitive fish (3)
13. Reasoned thought (5)
15. Department of France (capital: Bourg) (3)
17. Three legged island (3)
21. Cretan mountain (3)
23. Large flightless extinct bird (3)
24. Sturdy antelope (3)
19. For example (2)
22. Jamaican drink (3)

8.9	Minutes allowed	45
	Time taken	
	Points gained	

LOOK FOR THE K-WORDS

All answers begin with the letter K.

Answers

1. Mountain in Karakoram range
2. Island of south west Japan
3. Jewish blessing
4. U. S. Santa Claus
5. Native Hawaiian
6. Lakeland market town in England
7. Large prawn
8. One time Chancellor of Germany
9. South African desert
10. Scene of greatest volcanic eruption
11. Chinese martial art
12. Fate (Hindu)
13. Danish money
14. Sacred book of Islam
15. Moscow citadel

8.10	Minutes allowed	18
	Time taken	
	Points gained	

SIGNLESS SUM

Fill in the maths symbols (+, -, +, x) in the grid below so that all the numbers add up to 100. The signs are taken in order, as they occur, ignoring the mathematical rule of applying x and ÷ before + and -.

ANSWER:

8.11	Minutes allowed	15
	Time taken	
	Points gained	

NUMERO ROMANA

Fill in the grid below so that each vertical and horizontal line is a genuine Roman numeral. Here are the numerals you must use: 5 Cs, 7Xs, 1M, 3 Vs and 4 Is.

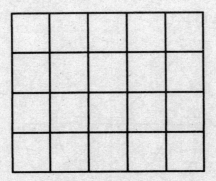

ANSWER:

8.12	Minutes allowed	**10**
	Time taken	
	Points gained	

CONCENTRIC CONCENTRATION

Place the numbers listed below into the diagram
so that each segment of three numbers adds up to
30, and each circle of 8 numbers adds up to 80.
The numbers you must use are: 14, 11, 10, 12, 7,
9, 9, 8, 9, 9, 11, 11, 10, 10, 10, 10, 14, 9, 7, 11,
10, 8, 12 and 9.

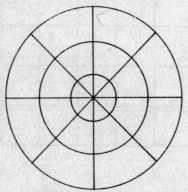

ANSWER:

8.13	Minutes allowed	10
	Time taken	
	Points gained	

PUNCHY PUZZLE

A punchy puzzle indeed! You must change the word FIST into the word HAND in as few moves as possible. Each move must produce a good English word.

F I S T

. . . .

. . . .

. . . .

. . . .

H A N D

ANSWER:

8.14

Minutes allowed	10
Time taken	
Points gained	

DIY CROSSWORD

The words down and across are given below, but you must decide where the blank squares are.

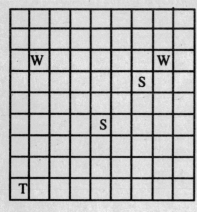

TEMPORARY T M
AWL   ISLET E I
SWEPT ARC L S
MALIGNANT E C
LENS   ITEM M R
OAST   ROLE E E
P   G   L   A   T   A
L   A   O   V   R   N
E   T   C   A   Y   T
A   E   U   S   Y   T
        M   T

S   L   L   N
I   I   E   I
L   E   A   T
O   S

	Minutes allowed	30
8.15	Time taken	
	Points gained	

ANSWERS

| | FOR CORRECT ANSWERS | | |
	Your Time	Time Allowed	Points Gained
8.1 Blocks of ice are arranged on the base so that the slings will go between them. The statue is placed on top of the blocks. When they melt the statue is on its base		10	
8.2 190		5	
8.3 Four: Trade, Tared, Rated and Dater		5	
8.4 680 revolutions		15	
8.5 5 symbols		10	
8.6 There were 6 customers; each painting cost £283		15	
8.7 138 goals. Adams scored 46, Brian scored 12, Chris scored 38, Dave scored 17 and Ed scored 25		10	
8.8 £38		8	
8.9 **Across 1.** Miracle worker **7.** Swanee whistle **9.** Coasts **11.** Ghee **12.** Lakeland **14.** Rang **16.** Homage **18.** Chenab **20.** Ionic **22.** Ram **24.** GDR **24.** Square measure			

CARRIED FORWARD

ANSWERS

	FOR CORRECT ANSWERS		
	Your Time	Time Allowed	Points Gained

BROUGHT FORWARD

			Time Allowed
8.9 (cont)	**Down 1.** Musical chairs **2.** Ria **3.** Cheat **4.** Eew **5.** Kit **6.** Riesengebirge **8.** Humid **10.** Ask **11.** Gar **13.** Logic **15.** Ain **17.** Man **19.** Eg **21.** Ida **22.** Rum **23.** Moa **24.** Gnu		45
8.10	K2. Kyushu. Kiddush. Kriss Kringle. Kanaka. Keswick. King Prawn. Kohl. Kalahari. Krakatoa. Kung Fu. Karma. Krone. Koran. Kremlin.		18
8.11	$5 + 7 - 2 \times 5 - 8 \times 2 - 4 + 4 \times 3 + 25 - 5 + 10 + 5 + 5$		15
8.12	M C C X X C C C X V X X X V I X V I I I		10
8.13	The outer circle contains the numbers in the following order: 7, 14, 9, 11, 9, 10, 8, 12. The middle ring: 14, 7, 11, 9, 10, 9, 12, 8. The outer ring: 9, 9, 10, 10, 11, 11, 10, 10		10

CARRIED FORWARD

ANSWERS

	FOR CORRECT ANSWERS		
	Your Time	Time Allowed	Points Gained

POINTS BROUGHT FORWARD

8.14	FIST, FAST, HAST, HART, HARD, HAND		10	
8.15	Answer below		30	

TOTAL POINTS GAINED

CHAPTER SUMMARY

Chapter Handicap Total:

Correct Answers x 5 points:

Chapter Total:

    Brought Forward:

    Running Total:

CHAPTER NINE

Target Time: 2 hours 51 minutes

FILL THE BLANK

Which letter should be placed in the blank square in the centre of this grid?

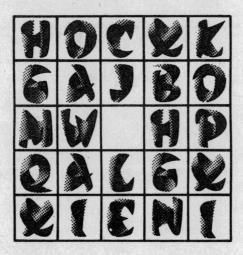

ANSWER:

9.1

Minutes allowed	15
Time taken	
Points gained	

SEEDY PUZZLE

A rather seedy puzzle, you might think! You must change the word SEED to the word TREE in as few moves as possible. Each change must produce a good English word.

S E E D

. . . .

. . . .

. . . .

. . . .

T R E E

ANSWER:

9.2	Minutes allowed	10
	Time taken	
	Points gained	

POST HASTE

Now can you change the word POST to the word MAIL in the same way. Each change must produce a good English word.

P O S T

· · · ·

· · · ·

· · · ·

· · · ·

M A I L

ANSWER:

9.3

Minutes allowed	10
Time taken	
Points gained	

CARRY IT ON

What letter should be used to continue the
following series?

F S T F F S S E

ANSWER:

	Minutes allowed	3
9.4	Time taken	
	Points gained	

INCOMPLETE XWORD

Here's another colourful puzzle. It's a magic square, with the first word written in. The words down and across are the same. Can you complete the square?

W H I T E
H
I
T
E

ANSWER:

9.5

Minutes allowed	10
Time taken	
Points gained	

AND ANOTHER

A not so colourful puzzle, but the same rules apply as for the previous one. Can you complete the square?

```
B   L   A   C   K
L
A
C
K
```

ANSWER:

9.6	Minutes allowed	10
	Time taken	
	Points gained	

THINK! USE YOUR BRAIN

THINK can become BRAIN by changing one letter at a time. Each alteration, however, must give a new acceptable word. What is the least number of changes you must make, and what are they?

ANSWER:

9.7	Minutes allowed	10
	Time taken	
	Points gained	

EVERY SECOND COUNTS

Find the letter which can replace the second letter in each of the words either side of the brackets in order to create two new words. Place this letter inside the brackets, and you will be able to read a newly formed word downwards. What is it?

SHORE	( )	ARE
SHOT	( )	BRAT
GOAT	( )	ODE
AGE	( )	INCH
FATE	( )	DIAL
AUK	( )	ACHES
SHEEP	( )	OUTER

ANSWER:

9.8	Minutes allowed	**10**
	Time taken	
	Points gained	

SYMBOL SEARCH

What are the missing symbols in the following calculation?

$$((5 \; ? \; 9) \; ? \; 4) \; ? \; 8 = 19.25$$

ANSWER:

9.9

Minutes allowed	5
Time taken	
Points gained	

THREE TO ONE AGAINST

How can you arrange three matches to equal one
– and not simply by putting them in a straight
vertical line?

ANSWER:

9.10	Minutes allowed	3
	Time taken	
	Points gained	

DOGGONE IT!

Select and re-arrange the letters from the sentence below to find the names of at least three types of dog.

I CAN STIR A MANAGER'S BLOOD

ANSWER:

9.11	Minutes allowed	10
	Time taken	
	Points gained	

AVERAGE IT OUT

An aeroplane maintains an average speed of 180 miles per hour from one airport to another. It then returns to the first airport over exactly the same distance at an average speed of 144 miles per hour. What was the average speed over the whole journey?

ANSWER:

9.12	Minutes allowed	5
	Time taken	
	Points gained	

HOW MANY WAYS?

How many different routes can you find from A to B by following the arrows?

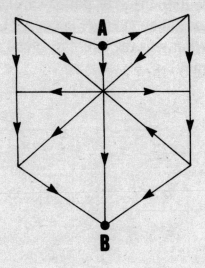

ANSWER:

9.13	Minutes allowed	15
	Time taken	
	Points gained	

SYMBOLIC NUMBERS

Once you have worked out the value of each of the symbols in the diagram below, you will be able to calculate the total which should replace the question mark. The figures at the end of each row and column are the total of the numbers represented by the symbols.

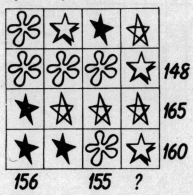

ANSWER:

9.14	Minutes allowed	10
	Time taken	
	Points gained	

DIY CROSSWORD

The words down and across are given below, but you must decide where the blank squares are.

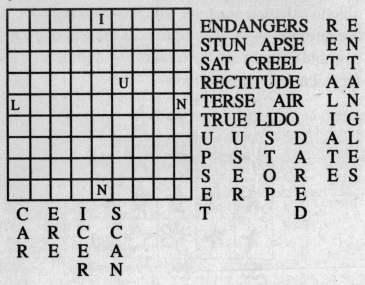

ENDANGERS   R   E
STUN APSE   E   N
SAT CREEL   T   T
RECTITUDE   A   A
TERSE AIR   L   N
TRUE LIDO   I   G
U   U   S   D   A   L
P   S   T   A   T   E
S   E   O   R   E   S
E   R   P   E
T   D   D

C   E   I   S
A   R   C   C
R   E   E   A
        R   N

9.15	Minutes allowed	45
	Time taken	
	Points gained	

ANSWERS

		FOR CORRECT ANSWERS		
		Your Time	Time Allowed	Points Gained
9.1	The missing letter is A. A = 10, B = 11, etc		15	
9.2	SEED, FEED, FLED, FLEE, FREE, TREE		10	
9.3	POST, MOST, MAST, MART, MARL, MAIL		10	
9.4	N. The series is the first letters of first, second, etc		3	
9.5	W H I T E H Y D R A I D I O T T R O V E E A T E N		10	
9.6	B L A C K L O G A N A G I L E C A L V E K N E E L		10	
9.7	THINK, THICK, TRICK, TRACK, TRACT, TRAIT, TRAIN, BRAIN		10	
9.8	The word is CONTEST		10	
9.9	The missing symbols are: "x", "+" and "+"		5	

CARRIED FORWARD

ANSWERS

	Your Time	Time Allowed	Points Gained

BROUGHT FORWARD

9.10

			3

9.11 The three dogs' names are: Alsatian, Corgi and Doberman — 10

9.12 160 mph — 5

9.13 There are 29 possible routes for getting from A to B — 15

9.14 162 — 10

9.15 See overleaf

CARRIED FORWARD

166

ANSWERS

FOR CORRECT ANSWERS

Your Time	Time Allowed	Points Gained

POINTS BROUGHT FORWARD

9.15 Answer below

| | 45 | |

TOTAL POINTS GAINED

R	E	C	T	I	T	U	D	E
E		A		C		P		N
T	E	R	S	E		S	A	T
A			T	R	U	E		A
L	I	D	O		S	T	U	N
I		A	P	S	E			G
A	I	R		C	R	E	E	L
T		E		A		R		E
E	N	D	A	N	G	E	R	S

CHAPTER SUMMARY

Chapter Handicap Total:

Correct Answers x 5 points:

Chapter Total:

Brought Forward:

Running Total:

CHAPTER
TEN

Target Time: 4 hours 0 minutes

UNBALANCED BRICKLAYER

Look at the illustration. Can such an unbalanced structure be built and sustained? I would not be asking if it could not be done. But how is is done? Using ordinary cubic bricks, no tricks. When the column is complete the vertical projection of the top brick must be entirely outside the perimeter of the bottom brick!

Table surface

ANSWER:

	Minutes allowed	20
10.1	Time taken	
	Points gained	

GEAR QUIZ

Imagine you have four cogs in constant mesh. The largest cog has 36 teeth, the second cog has 30 teeth, the third 24 teeth and the smallest 20 teeth. How many revolutions will the largest cog have to make before all the cogs return to their original positions?

ANSWER:

<table>
<tr><td rowspan="3" style="font-size:2em">**10.2**</td><td>Minutes allowed</td><td>**20**</td></tr>
<tr><td>Time taken</td><td></td></tr>
<tr><td>Points gained</td><td></td></tr>
</table>

DECODE THIS

Can you read the following quotation in code?
The vowels have been replaced with an 'X' and
the consonants have been replaced with a code
number.

20 9 X X 7   24 X 13 7 X 8 7 8   X 9 X 8 X
21 9 X 14   7 9 X 5 X X 15   7 19 X 13 20 8

ANSWER:

10.3	Minutes allowed	25
	Time taken	
	Points gained	

MAKE UP YOUR MINDS

Trace the letters of the word MIND in any order as many times as you can. You must always start at the centre 'M' and move from circle to touching circle. Once you have one set of letters you can count that and start again. Remember the letters can be collected in any order. How many different routes can you find?

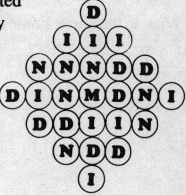

ANSWER:

10.4

Minutes allowed	20
Time taken	
Points gained	

LOSING TIME

Your watch was correct at midnight and, at that very moment, began to lose 16½ minutes every hour. When you look at the clock it is showing quarter past seven in the morning, and has stopped. In fact it stopped two hours ago.

What is the correct time?

ANSWER:

10.5	Minutes allowed	15
	Time taken	
	Points gained	

WEAVE BRAIN WAVE

In the grid below the letters of the word BRAINWAVE have been placed haphazardly in the square. By starting at the bottom 'B' and moving towards the top 'E' you will find more than one way of collecting all the letters of the word in any order. How many ways are there? By the way, you can not move diagonally.

N	W	W	V	E
I	N	W	A	V
A	I	N	W	A
R	A	I	N	W
B	R	A	I	N

ANSWER:

10.6	Minutes allowed	20
	Time taken	
	Points gained	

WHAT THE 'L'?

All answers begin with the letter 'L'

Answer

1. Barren elevated plain of Central Spain

2. River entering the Thames at Bromley-by-Bow

3. Seaside resort of Gwynedd featuring the Ormes

4. Capital of Bolivia

5. Arizona is the home of which once famous British bridge?

6. Priest who began the Reformation

7. British ship sunk in 1915 which encouraged US to join WW1

8. Mythical Cornish lost land

9. Discoverer of the use of antiseptics

10. Large-eyed primate found in Madagascar

11. Israeli political party of Yitzhak Shamir

12. Cretan writing deciphered by Ventris

10.7	Minutes allowed	15
	Time taken	
	Points gained	

MENSA XWORD

We have arranged the word MENSA so that it reads the same downwards as across. The intention is to complete the square so that it reads four more words across and down. The first will begin with the E of MENSA, the second with N, and so on.

Can you complete the square? The letters you must use are: EEEESSSSTTTLOODY

```
M E N S A
E
N
S
A
```

ANSWER:

10.8	Minutes allowed	20
	Time taken	
	Points gained	

CANDLEMAKER

You have 64 candle stubs in your possession. You can make one full candle from four stubs. A full candle burns for one hour. Imagine that you can only light full candles. Can you tell us what is the maximum number of hours you can expect to have candlelight from your supply?

ANSWER:

10.9	Minutes allowed	5
	Time taken	
	Points gained	

FIND THE WINNERS

In a lottery there are prizes worth in total $1,649. We know that each winner has won exactly the same value of prizes and that these are in full dollars only. There were more than 20 winners but fewer than 100. Can you tell us how many prize winners there are in all, and what the value of each prize is?

ANSWER:

10.10	Minutes allowed	10
	Time taken	
	Points gained	

BIKE SPEED

A famous motor cycle racing rider has taken delivery of his brand new turbo-charged motor bike. He "flies" down the track at a fantastic speed of 840 mph, hair streaming behind in the slip stream. He takes two hours on the trip, and then literally flies back to the start, covering exactly the same distance at a speed of 120 mph.

You have to work out his average speed for the whole journey, outward and return.

ANSWER:

10.11	Minutes allowed	5
	Time taken	
	Points gained	

SQUARE UP TO IT

Here is a word written both vertically and horizontally. Complete the word square in such a way that it reads both across and downwards with good English words.

```
F  O  R  T
O
R
T
```

ANSWER:

10.12	Minutes allowed	5
	Time taken	
	Points gained	

FIND THE SIGNS

Look at the following numbers. All the mathematical signs have been missed out. You have to replace them in such a way that the answer to the sum is 360.

23 ? 8 ? 7 ? 15 = 360

ANSWER:

10.13	Minutes allowed	**15**
	Time taken	
	Points gained	

USELESS TIMEPIECE

You have a mostv unreliable watch. It was correct at midnight, but at that very moment began to lose 40 minutes in every hour. It is now showing 2 am, but it stopped exactly five hours ago.

Can you tell us what the correct time is?

ANSWER:

10.14	Minutes allowed	15
	Time taken	
	Points gained	

DIY CROSSWORD

The words down and across are given below, but you must decide where the blank squares are.

I			N		L			S
						R		
				F				
T			N		W			D

MUFFINS POP
WEND ICON
PEEVE ARE
LASS SLIME
MUD RAN DIP
TERN ONE

SELFISH

ADORN UPPER SPAT IMPI SPEW

LEND SINE CURE ORE IRE ODE MAN

10.15	Minutes allowed	30
	Time taken	
	Points gained	

ANSWERS

	Your Time	Time Allowed	Points Gained

10.1   **Yes.** See illustration

Bottom block

At least three blocks

Top block

| | | 20 | |

10.2   The largest cog will have to make 60 revolutions

| | | 20 | |

10.3   The quotation is :
"Great contests arise from trivial things"

| | | 25 | |

10.4   There are 10 routes

| | | 20 | |

10.5   Midday

| | | 15 | |

10.6   There are 55 ways

| | | 20 | |

10.7   La Mancha. Lea (or Lee). Llandudno. La Paz. London. Luther. Lusitania. Lyonesse. Lister. Lemur. Likud. Linear B

| | | 15 | |

CARRIED FORWARD

ANSWERS

	FOR CORRECT ANSWERS	
Your Time	Time Allowed	Points Gained

BROUGHT FORWARD

10.8

```
M E N S A
E Y O T S
N O D E S
S T E L E
A S S E T
```
20

10.9 21 hours of candlelight. When you have used a candle the stub can be reused with others until each stub is used up — 5

10.10 There are 97 prize winners each with $17 in prizes — 10

10.11 Average speed is 210 mph — 5

10.12

```
F O R T
O L E O
R E N T
T O T E
```
5

10.13 $23 + 8 - 7 \times 15 = 360$ — 15

10.14 The correct time is 11 am — 15

10.15 See overleaf

CARRIED FORWARD

ANSWERS

FOR CORRECT ANSWERS

	Your Time	Time Allowed	Points Gained
POINTS BROUGHT FORWARD			
10.15 Answer below		30	
TOTAL POINTS GAINED			

CHAPTER SUMMARY

Chapter Handicap Total:	
Correct Answers x 5 points:	
Chapter Total:	
Brought Forward:	
Running Total:	

CHAPTER ELEVEN

Target Time: 3 hours 37 minutes

A SERIOUS PROBLEM

Here is a series of numbers. They are not random. Can you find the next two figures in the series, replacing the question marks. This is not an easy puzzle, because it is the interaction between a plurality of series.

5 8 11 14 17 23 27 32 35 41 49 52 ? ?

ANSWER:

11.1

Minutes allowed	15
Time taken	
Points gained	

PLANE RACE

In an air race over 100 km the Spitfire beat the Messerschmidt by exactly 10 kilometres. In order to show the British sense of fair play, the Spitfire then started 10 kilometres and 101 metres behind the start line. The race was then run again, and both planes maintained exactly the same speed as in the previous race.

Which one won this time?

ANSWER:

11.2	Minutes allowed	10
	Time taken	
	Points gained	

SALT INTO MINE

Can you go from SALT to MINE in only four moves, changing one letter at a time and always creating a good English word at each step?

S A L T

. . . .

. . . .

. . . .

M I N E

ANSWER:

11.3

Minutes allowed	10
Time taken	
Points gained	

MISQUOTATION

This Churchill quote has had all of the vowels removed. So from all of the consonants can you discover his pearl of wisdom?

GV S TH TLS, ND W SHLL FNSH TH JB

ANSWER:

11.4	Minutes allowed	5
	Time taken	
	Points gained	

COUNT YOUR DIAMONDS

Each like shape in the diagram has the same
value. The four numbers written above each
diamond represent the totals for the four shapes
within that particular diamond. The figure 133
represents the total value of the top line of eight
shapes. What is the value of the bottom eight
shapes?

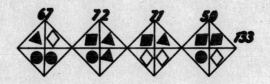

ANSWER:

11.5	Minutes allowed	12
	Time taken	
	Points gained	

IMMODESTY

An immodest sentence about this book is concealed below. The letters have been coded and all the vowels replaced with '?'. The code used follows the keys on a standard typewriter, i.e. A is at the top left and Z at the bottom right. What is the quote?

ZI? V?KSML D?LZ ?BES?L?CT ?FR
EI?SS?FU?FU H?MMS? W??A!

ANSWER:

11.6

Minutes allowed	10
Time taken	
Points gained	

TIMED CROSSWORD

Across

1. Wrote "The Raven" (5,5,3)
7. Used in printing crafts (7,6)
9. Mohandas K .... (6)
11. Where King John reputedly lost the Crown Jewels (4)
12. Nocturnal bird (8)
14. Scottish family (4)
16. Milfoil (6)
18. Resort of NE Italy (6)
20. Inert gas (5)
22. The Lion (3)
24. Oxygen, perhaps (3)
25. A score of greenbacks (6,7)

Down

1. Safety way out (11,4)
2. Greater London Council (3)
3. First Director Gen. of the BBC (5)
4. Cut up tree (3)
5. Houses engines on plane (3)
6. Disease causing extreme enlargement of affected areas (13)
8. The lowest point (5)
10. Egg based drink (3)
11. Terrestrial gathering of clerics (1,1,1)
13. Scottish town (5)
15. Garland (3)
17. Cricket score (3)
19. Doctor of Medicine (1,1)
21. Possess (3)
22. Electronics term (3)
23. Another nocturnal bird (3)
24. A kind of gazelle (3)

11.7	

Minutes allowed	45
Time taken	
Points gained	

WHERE IS YORKSHIRE?

The letters of the word YORKSHIRE have been set out in the diagram below. You must start at the bottom left hand letter, and move from circle to touching circle, collecting letters as you go. You must move upwards or across from left to right. How many different ways can you find of collecting the letters that create the word YORKSHIRE?

ANSWER:

11.8

Minutes allowed	8
Time taken	
Points gained	

WEAVE A SENTENCE

There is a sentence in the diagram below, in which the letters are placed in adjacent squares, each touching by a side or by just a corner. Your task is to find out where the sentence starts and what it says.

ANSWER:

11.9	Minutes allowed	18
	Time taken	
	Points gained	

THE PARTS OF A GLUTTON

Below you will find a sentence about a young man who ate and ate and ate. Within the sentence are hidden the five parts of his body which grew the fastest. Can you work out, using all the letters, what the five parts are?

HE SAT THERE AND HE FEASTED

ANSWER:

11.10	Minutes allowed	10
	Time taken	
	Points gained	

FIND THOSE WORDS

a) What word has 3 As, 3 Ls and a connection with letters?

2) Whilst GOING ABROAD you always go shopping and want a "........... ....".
What two words (4,7) that form an anagram of GOING ABROAD can be placed in the inverted commas?

ANSWER:

11.11	Minutes allowed	18
	Time taken	
	Points gained	

THE MAKING OF CUBES

Below is the cut out shape which can be used to create three of the cubes shown. Which three cubes cannot be made from this shape?

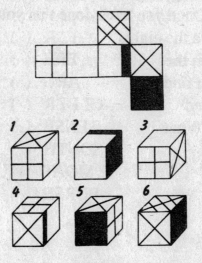

ANSWER:

11.12

Minutes allowed	8
Time taken	
Points gained	

LETTER CHANGE

For each pair of words below find the letter which can replace the first letter of both words to make to new words, and place it within the brackets. Once you have done this you must unscramble the eight letters from the brackets to find a long-tailed mammal. What is it?

FAR	( )	EVER
ERE	( )	IDES
ARC	( )	LILY
OLDER	( )	TASTER
TENSE	( )	DEEN
SOUTH	( )	KITE
MOAT	( )	PREEN
PURSE	( )	WEEDY

ANSWER:

11.13

Minutes allowed	10
Time taken	
Points gained	

STICKY BUNFIGHT

The sticky buns are back! The boss at your works party has invented a game to play with the sticky buns that the cleaner made. Here is the board, and you have to score a total of 56 points with 3 buns. The rules are that each bun must hit one of the figures on the board, each combination can be used once only, and you must stand eight feet away. How many ways are there to reach a total of 56?

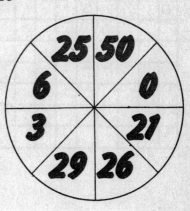

ANSWER:

11.14	Minutes allowed	8
	Time taken	
	Points gained	

DIY CROSSWORD

The words down and across are given below, but you must decide where the blank squares are.

		C						
O				O				
			O					
				C				
						O		

OASIS NUN
ORE AISLE
DECLINATE
ISLE MONK
ACNE OVER
TWITTERER

DEODORANT EASTERNER
SENOR CREME ORAL AKIN
IRON SKI ASS CENT

11.15		
	Minutes allowed	30
	Time taken	
	Points gained	

ANSWERS

	FOR CORRECT ANSWERS		
	Your Time	Time Allowed	Points Gained

11.1 The series arises from adding the prime numbers (top row) to the non-primes, in rising order, as follows:

1 2	3	5	7	11	13	17
4	6	8	9	10	12	14	15
5	8	11	14	17	23	27	32

19	23	29	31	37	41
16	18	20	21	22	24
35	41	49	52	**59**	**65**

15

11.2 Dead heat

10

11.3 SALT, MALT, MALE, MILE, MINE

10

11.4 "Give us the tools, and we shall finish the job"

5

11.5 127 (circle = 12, diamond = 18, triangle = 25 and rhombus = 10)

12

11.6 "The word's most exclusive and challenging puzzle book"

10

11.7 **Across 1.** Edgar Allen Poe
7. Etching needle
9. Ghandi **11.** Wash
12. Nightjar **14.** Clan
16. Yarrow **18.** Rimini

CARRIED FORWARD

ANSWERS

| | FOR CORRECT ANSWERS | | |
	Your Time	Time Allowed	Points Gained
	BROUGHT FORWARD		
11.7 (cont)	**Across 20.** Xenon **22.** Leo **24.** Gas **25.** Twenty dollars **Down 1.** Emergency exit **2.** GLC **3.** Reith **4.** Log **5.** Pod **6.** Elephantiasis **8.** Nadir **10.** Nog **11.** WCC (i.e. World Council of Churches) **13.** Troon **15.** Lei **17.** Run **19.** MD **21.** Own **22.** LED **23.** Owl **24.** Goa	45	
11.8	There are 9 ways of forming YORKSHIRE	8	
11.9	"Is yours big enough to join Mensa?"	18	
11.10	Teeth, Feet, Head, Ears, Hands	10	
11.11	a) Alphabetically b) Good bargain	18	
11.12	3, 4 and 6	8	
11.13	Mongoose	10	
11.14	There are 4 ways of scoring 56	8	
	CARRIED FORWARD		

ANSWERS

POINTS BROUGHT FORWARD

11.15   Answer below | | 30

TOTAL POINTS GAINED

CHAPTER SUMMARY

Chapter Handicap Total:

Correct Answers x 5 points:

Chapter Total:

Brought Forward:

Running Total:

CHAPTER TWELVE

Target Time: 3 hours 55 minutes

HOW FAST?

a) A car travels a distance of 100 miles at a speed of 65 mph. It covers 25 miles per gallon, and has a total tank capacity of 9 gallons. However, sod's law strikes again, and the petrol tank has sprung a leak. It was full when the car set off, but is empty when the car reaches its destination. How much fuel has it lost per hour?

b) You are on a train travelling at only $9^1/2$ mph due to the fact that it is $3/4$ mile long. It enters a tunnel which is $9^1/2$ miles long, and keeps to its constant speed. How long will it take for the train to pass completely through the tunnel?

ANSWER:

12.1	Minutes allowed	25
	Time taken	
	Points gained	

LONGEST WORD

What is the longest word with a connection with the elements which begins with 'A', ends with 'M' and contains the letter 'U'?

ANSWER:

12.2	Minutes allowed	3
	Time taken	
	Points gained	

LEGS? – OR WHAT?

If a goat has got four legs, an elephant 6, a peacock 6 and an alsatian 8 – how many legs has an octopus?

ANSWER:

12.3	Minutes allowed	5
	Time taken	
	Points gained	

A SQUARE LAKE

Fill in the spaces in the grid below to complete the word square with three more words which read both across and down.

L	A	K	E
A	A		
K		K	-
E			E

ANSWER:

12.4

Minutes allowed	10
Time taken	
Points gained	

IS IT SAFE?

Here is a diagram of the new security lock keypad on your office safe. You urgently need to gain access to the safe in order to get your hands on the £10,000 stored there. But all you know about the combination is that you can press the buttons that are joined by a thin black line, and must find a combination that adds up to 22. How many ways are there of reaching this total?

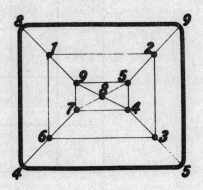

ANSWER:

12.5	Minutes allowed	10
	Time taken	
	Points gained	

ALTERED SAYING

Find the starting letter in this grid, and by moving one square at a time discover the hidden misquotation. The following riddle is a clue: "In a far off country wool is washed in one stream after another. One wool washer was too enthusiastic however. His cloth shrunk!" The coiled sentence will give the moral of the story.

X	O	P	O	I
T	O	S	L	T
A	M	S	H	E
Y	N	K	L	C
B	R	O	O	Z
Z	O	T	H	X

ANSWER:

12.6

Minutes allowed	10
Time taken	
Points gained	

DESTRUCTION! NO!

The self destruct button on the Inter-Galactic shuttle has been armed. You know that to stop it you have to make the smallest total possible by pressing five buttons in order, folowing the thin black lines. Each button has a value shown in the diagram, and you must deactivate the self destruct. What combination of five buttons will give the smallest total?

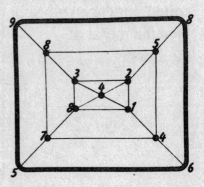

ANSWER:

12.7	Minutes allowed	**10**
	Time taken	
	Points gained	

EXCHANGE OF LETTERS

Replace the first letter of each of the words either side of the brackets with another letter which will make two new, good English words. Place this letter inside the brackets, and once all the letters have been entered you will find another word, which will be very educational for you.

LUNG ( ) FUN
FAKE ( ) PAGE
MUDDLE ( ) CALF
NIL ( ) CUT
ARE ( ) INSET
HOG ( ) HOW

ANSWER:

12.8	Minutes allowed	10
	Time taken	
	Points gained	

STAINED GLASS AND BRICKS

Here we have a stained glass window made from unbreakable glass. Local hooligans are challenged to test its strength by throwing bricks at it. Each hooligan is allowed to throw 5 bricks and must hit five different panes to score a total of 250. Assuming every hooligan achieves this degree of accuracy, how many would be needed to achieve every possible combination? I.e. once a group of five numbers has been used it cannot be reused in a different order.

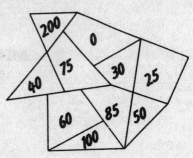

ANSWER:

12.9

Minutes allowed	20
Time taken	
Points gained	

A QUESTION OF BALANCE

Here are some arithmetical signs placed on a set of scale pans. The first two sets are perfectly balanced. How many multiplication signs should be put on the bottom scales in order to balance them? Fractions of a sign are allowed.

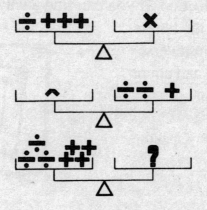

ANSWER:

12.10

Minutes allowed	15
Time taken	
Points gained	

MAKING WAVES

Look at the diagram and tell us how many
different ways you can find of collecting the
letters of the word WAVES, following these
instructions. You must start at a corner and
follow the lines, and can only include one corner
in each selection. If you can find a way of
collecting the letters
twice but in reverse
order, you can count
that as two.

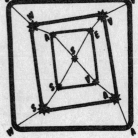

ANSWER:

12.11	Minutes allowed	15
	Time taken	
	Points gained	

BOOZER'S SWAP

Wine is wine and beer is beer, or so you would think! Well, I know someone who can change wine into beer in six easy steps. Changing one letter at a time, and always creating a new good English word, can you do the same – or even better?

```
W  I  N  E
·  ·  ·  ·
·  ·  ·  ·
·  ·  ·  ·
·  ·  ·  ·
·  ·  ·  ·
B  E  E  R
```

ANSWER:

12.12	Minutes allowed	15
	Time taken	
	Points gained	

TIMED CROSSWORD

Across

1. Works with a doll (13)
7. An Ascot prophet? (6,7)
9. Kind of beetle (6)
11. Roughage (4)
12. Neapolitan resort (8)
14. Nought (4)
16. Given in fulfilment of a vow (6)
18. Caviar (6)
20. Inside (5)
22. Curve (3)
24. Mongrel (3)
25. Rulers (8,5)

Down

1. Painful leg ailment (8,5)
2. Birmingham show place (1,1,1)
3. Large grazing area (5)
4. He had a salty wife (3)
5. International cut short (3)
6. Extinct large lizard (13)
8. Adult mature insect (5)
10. Tune (3)
11. Dickens, perhaps (3)
13. Young eel (5)
15. Large bird (3)
17. Cask of wine (3)
19. American town (1,1)
21. Long period of time (3)
22. Tree (3)
23. British athlete (3)
24. Toothed wheel (3)

12.13	Minutes allowed	45
	Time taken	
	Points gained	

QUIZ

Answers

1. Name the 1951 film which featured Ronald Reagan as a chimp.

2. In which city did John F Kennedy die?

3. Name the character who ran away when the boys came out to play.

4. Name the first day of the week.

5. Which sport begins in front of the south stake?

6. Which two countries have their flags flying over Caribbean Virgins?

7. Who wrote "Death on the Nile"?

8. How many Queen bees reign in in bee hive?

9. In which street was the bakery that started the Great Fire of London?

10. Where is the Trevi fountain?

11. Who was the founder of Islam?

12. Who was the first woman to fly solo across the Atlantic?

12.14	Minutes allowed	12
	Time taken	
	Points gained	

DIY CROSSWORD

The words down and across are given below, but you must decide where the blank squares are.

								R
	I							
				R				
	I							
			W					Y

HERON PIN C
AGE ALONE H
STARTER A
APE GREY R
STEW ODD G
DIN STIR E
SCAR ROD R
I S E E W R
N P R D A E
E A R D D N
P R O Y S T
L O C T O A T R
I D A I N G
T E R P E O

12.15	Minutes allowed	**30**
	Time taken	
	Points gained	

ANSWERS

		Your Time	Time Allowed	Points Gained
12.1	a) 3.25 gallons			
	b) 64 mins, 44 sec		25	
12.2	Aluminium		3	
12.3	6 legs (2 for each vowel)		5	
12.4	L A K E A P E S K E E P E S P Y		10	
12.5	There are two ways: 8+1+6+3+4=22 4+6+3+4+5=22		10	
12.6	"Too many brooks spoil the cloth"		10	
12.7	6+4+1+2+3=16		10	
12.8	SCHOOL		10	
12.9	You will need 39 hooligans because there are 39 different ways of scoring 250		20	
12.10	One and a half multiplication signs		15	
12.11	There are six different ways of making the word WAVE		15	

CARRIED FORWARD

ANSWERS

BROUGHT FORWARD

12.12 WINE, WIND, WEND, BEND, BEAD, BEAR, BEER

15

12.13. **Across 1.** Ventriloquist
7. Racing tipster
9. Chafer **11.** Bran
12. Sorrento **14.** Zero
16. Votive **18.** Beluga
20. Inner **22.** Arc **24.** Cur
25. Straight edges
Down 1. Varicose veins
2. N.E.C. **3.** Range
4. Lot **5.** Int **6.** Tyranno-
saurus **8.** Imago **10.** Air
11. Boz **13.** Elver
15. Emu **17.** Tun **19.** LA
21. Era **22.** Ash **23.** Coe
24. Cog

45

12.14 **1.** "Bedtime for Bonzo"
2. Dallas **3.** Georgie
Porgie **4.** Sunday
5. Croquet **6.** The US
and Britain **7.** Agatha
Christie **8.** One
9. Pudding Lane
10. Rome **11.** Mohammed
12. Amelia Earhart

12

CARRIED FORWARD

ANSWERS

	FOR CORRECT ANSWERS		
	Your Time	Time Allowed	Points Gained
POINTS BROUGHT FORWARD			
12.15 Answer below			30
TOTAL POINTS GAINED			

CHAPTER SUMMARY

Chapter Handicap Total:

Correct Answers x 5 points:

Chapter Total:

Brought Forward:

Running Total:

CHAPTER THIRTEEN

Target Time: 2 hours 19 minutes

PAST AND PRESENT

Hyacinth Seer claims that she has immediate sensory perception of past events. Jock Sceptic says fiddle-dee-dee, the only events we can directly perceive are events of immediate experience.

Strictly speaking, which of them is right, if any?

ANSWER:

13.1	Minutes allowed	**3**
	Time taken	
	Points gained	

NESTING TETRAHEDRA

A Rubic Cube is made up of 27 nested cubes. Here is a Rubik tretrahedron or four-faced pyramid. If it is made up of units inside consistent with its external appearance, how many tetrahedra does it contain?

ANSWER:

	Minutes allowed	10
13.2	Time taken	
	Points gained	

COMBINATION

Here is a combination lock to the postal bag that the young cashier has to take to the post office. It can be opened by putting the key into the correct locks in order. You can only follow the thin black lines, and the combination must add up to 63. How many different combinations are there?

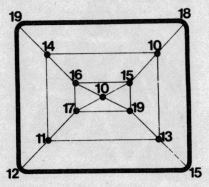

ANSWER:

13.3

Minutes allowed	5
Time taken	
Points gained	

SIGN IN

Look at the following numbers. All the mathematical signs have been missed out. You have to replace them to get the answer 97.

$$32 \; ? \; 12 \; ? \; 4 \; ? \; 1 = 97$$

ANSWER:

13.4	Minutes allowed	5
	Time taken	
	Points gained	

SHARING THE SHOES

The stables were trying to get rid of their old horse shoes. They had 2156 to get rid of, and they knew that a group of people would want them. They had to make sure that each person got the same number of shoes. There were over 78 people involved but under one hundred.

How many people received horse shoes, and how many did they each receive?

ANSWER:

13.5

Minutes allowed	5
Time taken	
Points gained	

CRAZY CLOCK

The alarm clock has gone crazy. It was correct at midnight but immediately began to lose twelve minutes per hour. It now shows one o'clock in the morning, but it actually stopped ten hours ago.

You should be at work for ten o'clock that morning. Will you be late?

ANSWER:

13.6	Minutes allowed	5
	Time taken	
	Points gained	

FIT THE DIGITS

This is a magic square, with all of the numbers left out. We are going to give them to you in a moment, and you must fill them in so that each horizontal and vertical line and the two main diagonals add up to 125. Here are the numbers:

One 1, one 9, one 18,
two 20s, two21s,
two 23s, two 24s,
two 25s, two 26s,
two 27s, two 29s,
three 30s, one 38
and one 52.

ANSWER:

13.7	Minutes allowed	15
	Time taken	
	Points gained	

SQUARE IT

Here is a word written both vertically and horizontally. Complete the word square in such a way that it reads the same both across and down with just four good English words.

B O N E
O
N
E

ANSWER:

13.8	Minutes allowed	**10**
	Time taken	
	Points gained	

AND AGAIN

Here is another word square but this time there are five letters instead of four. Can you complete it with four more good English words that read both horizontally and vertically?

```
T H R O W
H Q a v e
R A v e l
O v e r s
W e l s h
```

ANSWER:

13.9	Minutes allowed	12
	Time taken	
	Points gained	

238

LETTER SWITCH

Replace the first letter of each pair of words, either side of the brackets, with another letter which will form two new good English words, and place this letter in the brackets. When you read all the letters in the brackets you will find another word. What is it?

WIND ( ) CAP
AVER ( ) BATH
MACE ( ) RACK
SATIN ( ) DEMON
TOUR ( ) LAWN

ANSWER:

13.10	Minutes allowed	10
	Time taken	
	Points gained	

239

STEAL A LETTER

The same letter, which occurs at least three times
in each of the following words, has been
removed from them, and the remaining letters
mixed up. Can you find the missing letter and
unscramble the words?

TMRNC
JHRHM
LICTNF
PRISLP
NTLRCH

ANSWER:

13.11

Minutes allowed	8
Time taken	
Points gained	

FROM PAPER TO NOVEL

Can you turn PAPER into NOVEL in only six steps, changing one letter at a time? Of course, each change must result in the creation of another completely acceptable word.

P A P E R

· · · · ·

· · · · ·

· · · · ·

· · · · ·

· · · · ·

N O V E L

ANSWER:

13.12	Minutes allowed	8
	Time taken	
	Points gained	

CHANGE, MAKE

If you change the second letter of each of the pairs of words shown, and place the new letter you have used in the brackets between the words, you will create a new word reading downwards. You must create two new words either side of the brackets.

SLOP ( ) SMART
SLAM ( ) CRIME
ALL ( ) BAND
ORES ( ) ORYX
SLATE ( ) SHIN

ANSWER:

13.13

Minutes allowed	8
Time taken	
Points gained	

DISENVOWELLED

The following well-known quotation has had all the vowels removed, and the remaining letters have been broken up into groups of five (except the last one, because there weren't five letters left!). Put back the vowels and find the quotation.

RSBYN YTHRN MWLDS MLLSS WT

ANSWER:

13.14

Minutes allowed	5
Time taken	
Points gained	

DIY CROSSWORD

The words down and across are given below, but you must decide where the blank squares are.

				V				
	W					V		
U								
				W				

VAN WASTE S P
SWEET ADO E O
USES REST N S
LOBE ELSE S T
ELECTRICS E U
PARAVANES L L
N E S V E A
O R W E S T
V O A T S E
E D T O
L E B E
S R E L
K O T S
I E A E

13.15	Minutes allowed	30
	Time taken	
	Points gained	

ANSWERS

	FOR CORRECT ANSWERS		
	Your Time	Time Allowed	Points Gained

13.1 Strictly speaking Hyacinth is right. We can only know the past because the movement of information takes time, and perception itself takes processing time. — 3 —

13.2 Tetrahedra will not nest like cubes. The Rubik tetrahedron is made up of 4 octahedra and 11 tetrahedra, one of which is right in the centre, nested between the 5 octahedra. — 10 —

13.3 There are 4 combinations — 5 —

13.4 32 x 12 ÷ 4 + 1 = 97 — 5 —

13.5 There were 98 people who each received 22 horse shoes — 5 —

13.6 Yes, you will be late. It is really 11.15 a.m. — 5 —

13.7
27 38 29 01 30
18 29 26 27 25
30 26 25 24 20
30 23 24 21 27
20 09 21 52 23 — 15 —

CARRIED FORWARD

ANSWERS

		FOR CORRECT ANSWERS	
	Your Time	Time Allowed	Points Gained

BROUGHT FORWARD

13.8
```
B O N E
O M E N
N E E D
E N D S
```
10

13.9
```
T H R O W
H E A V E
R A V E L
O V E R S
W E L S H
```
12

13.10   The word is HOLLY   10

13.11   The missing letter is A
The words are:
CATAMARAN
MAHARAJAH
FANATICAL
APPRAISAL
CHARLATAN   8

13.12   PAPER, PAVER, CAVER,
COVER, HOVER,
HOVEL, NOVEL   8

13.13   THINK   8

13.14   "A rose by any other name
would smell as sweet"   5

CARRIED FORWARD

ANSWERS

	Your Time	*Time Allowed*	*Points Gained*
POINTS BROUGHT FORWARD			
13.15 Answer below		30	
TOTAL POINTS GAINED			

CHAPTER SUMMARY

Chapter Handicap Total:

Correct Answers x 5 points:

Chapter Total:

Brought Forward:

Running Total:

CHAPTER
FOURTEEN

Target Time: 3 hours 14 minutes

BORING BALL

A perfect sphere has a cylindrical hole bored through its centre. The empty cylinder within is exactly 100mm long, and that is all you may know. You are not permitted to know the diameter of the hole, nor that of the sphere. Yet you have enough information to deduce the volume of the remaining perforated sphere. What is it?

The formula for the volume of a sphere is: $(4 \times \pi \times r^3)/3$. For a cylinder it is $l \times \pi \times r^2$, where l = length and r = radius. Calculators may be used.

ANSWER:

14.1	Minutes allowed	**15**
	Time taken	
	Points gained	

TAKE AND MAKE

By removing one letter – the same letter – from both words either side of the brackets and then placing that letter in the brackets, you can form a word reading vertically. Remember that when you remove the letter from each of the words you must leave a new word which can be found in the dictionary.

STRAWY ( ) WHALE
WRAITH ( ) SLEIGHT
MANNED ( ) EVEN
BARED ( ) DROVER
SHIP ( ) LIST

ANSWER:

14.2	Minutes allowed	10
	Time taken	
	Points gained	

HELP THE BIRD TO NEST

Can you go from BIRD to NEST in six changes, changing only one letter each time, and making a new, acceptable English word at each change?

B I R D

. . . .

. . . .

. . . .

. . . .

. . . .

N E S T

ANSWER:

14.3	Minutes allowed	**10**
	Time taken	
	Points gained	

WHATEVER WORDS?

The following combinations of letters are quite unusual, but each one is part of a word – exactly as it appears in that word. You have to discover what the four words are.

XYG   XOP   WKW   YZY

ANSWER:

14.4	Minutes allowed	10
	Time taken	
	Points gained	

CAN YOU FOLD THE BOX?

This work box has been flattened out. A number of made up work boxes can be found at the foot of the flattened out pattern. Can you tell us which four of the completed boxes cannot be constructed from the pattern?

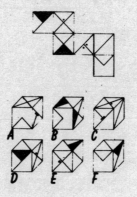

ANSWER:

14.5	Minutes allowed	8
	Time taken	
	Points gained	

DIZZY DISCOUNTS

A travel agent is offering discounts on flights to various islands. The discount is calculated by their name. With the information of this board can you tell us how many pounds discount there is on a flight to the Falklands?

CRETE	15
JERSEY	20
MALTA	15
CANARY	20
FALKLANDS	?

ANSWER:

14.6

Minutes allowed	8
Time taken	
Points gained	

LEAKY

There is a fire exactly 34 miles away. The fire engine, travelling at exactly 60 mph, holds exactly 1000 gallons of water. However, someone left the hose on the last time they went to a fire and it is pumping out water at a speed of 25 gallons per minute. It is only a small fire and will need 125 gallons to put it out. Will the fire engine arrive there with enough water to put out the fire?

ANSWER:

14.7	Minutes allowed	12
	Time taken	
	Points gained	

FAG END FACTORY

The tramp with his portable "cigarette stub conversion unit" (or CSCU for short) has found a large stash of stubs hidden by one of his local rivals. He can make one whole cigarette from seven stubs and in the stash there are 1,498 stubs.

How many full cigarettes can he make in total?

ANSWER:

14.8	Minutes allowed	12
	Time taken	
	Points gained	

COLLECT 'EM

Here is a grid of numbers. You have to start from the bottom left hand corner and finish in the top right hand corner. You can move upwards or from left to right collecting numbers as you go and adding them together. What is the lowest possible score, and how many different ways can you go from start to finish with a score of 46?

5 6 2 3 5
6 2 3 5 6
2 3 5 6 2
3 5 6 2 3
start 5 6 2 3 5

ANSWER:

14.9

Minutes allowed	20
Time taken	
Points gained	

CHRISTMAS SHAREOUT

The local garage gave away $3,395 at Christmas to its top account holding customers. There were more than 50 such customers but less than 100, and each one received an equal amount in whole dollars only.

What was the amount, and how many customers were there?

ANSWER:

14.10	Minutes allowed	15
	Time taken	
	Points gained	

TRAVEL TROUBLE

A man sets out to travel from one town to another. On the first day he covers one half of the total distance. On the second day he covers one third of the remaining distance. On the third day he covers one third of the remaining distance and on the fourth day he covers one half of the remaining distance.

He now has 37 miles left to reach the second town. What distance has he travelled so far?

ANSWER:

14.11	Minutes allowed	12
	Time taken	
	Points gained	

PINBALL SCORE

Here is a small pinball machine. You have five moves along the thin black lines, starting from one of the outside corners. What is the lowest total you can achieve counting a corner and four other scores, and from which corner must you start to achieve it?

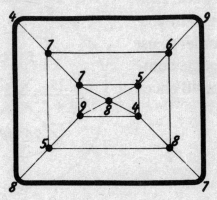

ANSWER:

14.12	Minutes allowed	10
	Time taken	
	Points gained	

DARTS SCORE

From the same games package as the pinball machine came a small dartboard with only nine segments and a set of *four* darts. You have to use the four darts and score 40 points. We will take it that you are a good shot and none of the darts miss the board. How many darts will you throw in order to use every possible combination of 40 once only?

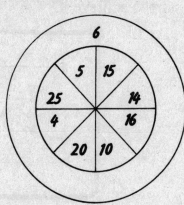

ANSWER:

14.13

Minutes allowed	12
Time taken	
Points gained	

HANDICAP

In a 100-yard race Miss Cawthorne beats Miss Topham by 9 yards. The race is then re-run with the winner or the last race starting 9 yards behind the start line. If they maintain the same form as in the previous race, who will win this time?

ANSWER:

14.14	Minutes allowed	10
	Time taken	
	Points gained	

DIY CROSSWORD

The words down and across are given below, but
you must decide where the blank squares are.

S								B
W								
				A				
B								S

RELATED   B
SEDAN   PIN   B E
ACE   ENDUE   C
SLOB   BEDS   A
STAY   FEES   U
ARE   RID   L E   S
OLD   NET   A N   E
A   O   D   N D
L   R   O   C E
E   E   E   E D

C   B   S   E   A   T   I
R   E   P   N   N   I   C
A   T   E   D   D   N   E
B   A   W   S

14.15	Minutes allowed	30
	Time taken	
	Points gained	

ANSWERS

	Your Time	Time Allowed	Points Gained
14.1 This can be solved by elaborate calculation or by commonsense. If the solver does not need to know the diameter of the hole it must be irrelevant. So assume it is zero. We then have a sphere of radius 50mm with a volume from our formula of 523,598.78mm		15	
14.2 WINDS		10	
14.3 BIRD, BARD, BAND, BEND, BENT, BEST, NEST		10	
14.4 Oxygen, Saxophone, Awkward, Syzygy		10	
14.5 A, C, E & F cannot be made		8	
14.6 £35 (£5 per consonant)		8	
14.7 Yes		12	
14.8 248 cigarettes		12	
14.9 The lowest number is 28 which can be achieved only once. 46 can be scored seven ways		20	

CARRIED FORWARD

ANSWERS

		FOR CORRECT ANSWERS	
	Your Time	Time Allowed	Points Gained

BROUGHT FORWARD

14.10	97 people each receive $35		15	
14.11	The man has travelled 296 miles so far		12	
14.12	The lowest possible score is 26, and is reached by starting from the top left hand corner		10	
14.13	There are sixteen combinations that add up to 40, which multiplied by the four darts gives an answer of 64		12	
14.14	Miss Cawthorne will again win the race		10	
14.15	See overleaf			

CARRIED FORWARD

ANSWERS

POINTS BROUGHT FORWARD

14.15 Answer below | | 30

TOTAL POINTS GAINED

CHAPTER SUMMARY

Chapter Handicap Total:

Correct Answers x 5 points:

Chapter Total:

Brought Forward:

Running Total:

CHAPTER
FIFTEEN

Target Time: 2 hours 35 minutes

BACK-PEDAL PROBLEM

A free-standing bicycle is placed on a firm road. Someone lightly hold the bike so that it is free to move. You kneel and push on the pedal as shown in the drawing, pushing the pedal backwards. Does the bike move forwards or backwards?

ANSWER:

15.1	Minutes allowed	3
	Time taken	
	Points gained	

SPACE TRAVEL TIME

You are time travelling, using the map below. The black dots mark time tunnels which take you back 8 years in time; the white dots take you forward by the number of years indicated. Starting in 1949 you must attempt to travel as far into the future as possible, following the directions indicated by the arrows. In what year will you emerge?

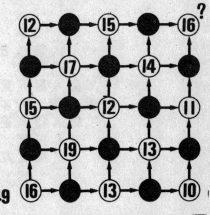

1949

ANSWER:

15.2	Minutes allowed	12
	Time taken	
	Points gained	

THE FLOWER IN MAY

There are some May flowers in the diagram below, but how many? You have to move from the bottom M to the top R and discover how many ways you can form the words MAY FLOWER, by moving diagonally upwards only.

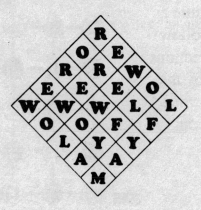

ANSWER:

15.3	Minutes allowed	12
	Time taken	
	Points gained	

SYMBOL STRING

Look at the string of symbols below, and work out why they are strung like this. Having done that, tell us what the next symbol should be.

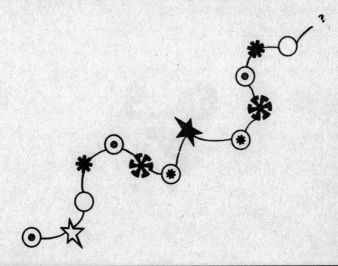

ANSWER:

15.4

Minutes allowed	12
Time taken	
Points gained	

ENDLESS ESPRIT

How many English words can you make from the following five letters. Each letter must be used in the word, but can be used once only.

ANSWER:

15.5	Minutes allowed	10
	Time taken	
	Points gained	

BULL CHASES JOGGER

A jogger was crossing a green pasture on a pleasant spring day when he caught sight of a magnificent black bull. Unfortunately the bull also caught sight of him. The jogger's speed increased to a steady 48mph until he reached the fence. Just as he was about to leap over it he noticed that on the other side was a 2000ft drop into the sea.

Having no time to change into swimming gear, he did a rapid U-turn, passing the bull on his way. On the way back his average speed was 32mph. The bull's average speed in both directions was 40 mph. Did it catch him?

ANSWER:

15.6	Minutes allowed	15
	Time taken	
	Points gained	

RUNS? INNINGS?

A cricketer scores an average of sixteen runs in his first 15 innings. Brilliant play! He then has a further ten innings, and his batting average per innings increases to eighteen.

What was his average for the last ten innings?

ANSWER:

15.7

Minutes allowed	12
Time taken	
Points gained	

RABBITS, CARROTS

Each of the diamond shaped fields in the diagram below contains a number of carrots. This number is displayed in the field for the benefit of short-sighted rabbits. Moving from the bottom field with 14 carrots to the top field with 13 carrots, and only moving from field to touching field diagonally upwards, what it the maximum number of carrots that the rabbits can eat?

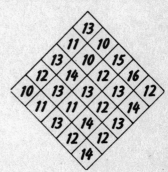

ANSWER:

15.8

Minutes allowed	12
Time taken	
Points gained	

COLLECT 'EM UP

Starting at the centre square and moving outwards in any direction, collect just four numbers which add up to 48. You can only move from square to touching square vertically or horizontally, not diagonally. How many ways are there of reaching this total?

			15			
		12	15	5		
	5	12	15	12	5	
12	15	12	16	5	12	15
	15	5	5	15	12	
		5	12	15		
			12			

ANSWER:

15.9	Minutes allowed	12
	Time taken	
	Points gained	

WHAT'S THE LOGIC HERE?

Logic prevails here! The letters at the points of the triangles are all there for some logical reason, which isn't difficult to fathom out. Which letter should replace the question mark?

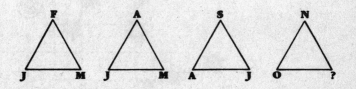

ANSWER:

15.10	Minutes allowed	5
	Time taken	
	Points gained	

ANOTHER SYMBOL STRING

Look at this string of symbols and work out why they are strung like this. Having done that, tell us what the next symbol should be. This one's so easy the dog's just done it!

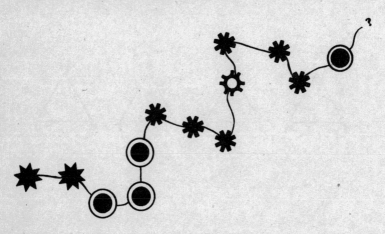

ANSWER:

15.11	Minutes allowed	5
	Time taken	
	Points gained	

ROMAN SQUARES

Below is a series of squares adorned with Roman numerals. You have to work out the logic of the series and tell us what should appear inside the last square to replace the question mark.

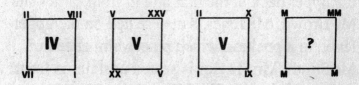

ANSWER:

15.12

Minutes allowed	5
Time taken	
Points gained	

SEATING ARRANGEMENTS

The two-decker minibus has five seats upstairs and five downstairs. You can see that Mrs Black is sitting behind Mr Green, while Mr Roberts is sitting in the front of the bus in front of Mr Smith. Mrs White – she's fainted – is slumped on the upper deck at the rear and in front of her sits Mr Brown. Mr Jones is also seated on the upper level, in a position which places him ahead of Mr Smith. Mrs Taylor is seated upstairs in front of Mrs Peters, who is sitting above Mr Green. Assuming that all the seats are occupied and that the last passenger is Mrs Grey, where is she sitting?

ANSWER:

15.13	Minutes allowed	5
	Time taken	
	Points gained	

RECOMBINE

There are quite a few rides here. You have to work out just how many. A letter can be used more than once and is regarded as being different, but once a combination of letters has been used it cannot be used again in any order.

Thus there may be two Rs, but they are regarded as being different letters. Got it? Start counting and ride out to victory!

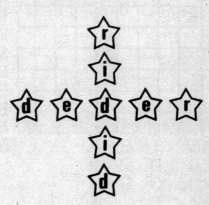

ANSWER:

15.14	Minutes allowed	5
	Time taken	
	Points gained	

DIY CROSSWORD

The words down and across are given below, but you must decide where the blank squares are.

								K
						M		
K								
	Q							Y

TAMED	BUS	S	E
AGO	AMEND	O	N
SHELDRAKE		A	D
DEAR	TRUE	K	L
RISE	AREA	A	E
SQUALIDLY		W	S
R	E	D	E	A	S
E	R	A	A	Y	L
B	O	T	R	S	Y
I	D	A	N		
D	E	A	N		

A I E A
I D M R
M O U T
   L U S

ANSWERS

	Your Time	Time Allowed	Points Gained
15.1 The bicycle will go backwards. This is a relativity problem. Because of the gear ratio when you are riding forwards, the bottom pedal goes backwards relative to the bike, but forwards relative to the ground. So if you push the lower pedal backwards, the bike goes backwards		3	
15.2 The year 2000. The further distance is 51 years		12	
15.3 You can form the words MAY FLOWER 5 ways		12	
15.4 Large white star		12	
15.5 Piers. Prise. Pries. Spire		10	
15.6 More than likely, since the jogger's average speed is 38.4 mph		15	
15.7 21 runs		12	
15.8 120 carrots		12	
15.9 You can reach a total of 48 in 11 ways		12	

CARRIED FORWARD

ANSWERS

BROUGHT FORWARD

		Time Allowed	
15.10	The missing letter is D. The letters are the initial letters of the 12 months	5	
15.11	The black and white circle	5	
15.12	The missing Roman numeral is II	5	
15.13	Mrs Grey is sitting at the rear downstairs	5	
15.14	There are 24 ways of forming the word RIDE	5	
15.15			

S	H	E	L	D	R	A	K	E
O		R		A		I		N
A	G	O		T	A	M	E	D
K		D	E	A	R			L
A	R	E	A		T	R	U	E
W			R	I	S	E		S
A	M	E	N	D		B	U	S
Y		M		O		I		L
S	Q	U	A	L	I	D	L	Y

30

TOTAL POINTS GAINED

ANSWERS

CHAPTER SUMMARY

Chapter Handicap Total:	
Correct Answers x 5 points:	
Chapter Total:	
Brought Forward:	
Running Total:	

CHAPTER SIXTEEN

Target Time: 2 hours 45 minutes

SQUARING THE PYRAMID

This is a test of 3D visual imagination. Picture a tetrahedron made of wood. Can you saw through it with one straight plane cut so that the two sawn surfaces you have exposed make two perfect squares on a flat plane? Well, can you?

ANSWER:

16.1

Minutes allowed	5
Time taken	
Points gained	

WAITING FOR THE BATH

It takes one tap twelve minutes to fill a bath, whilst it takes the other six minutes to fill it up. The plug has been left out, however, and the bath will empty in eight minutes.

If both taps are on full and the plug is left out, how long will it take for the bath to fill up, if it will fill up at all?

ANSWER:

16.2	Minutes allowed	10
	Time taken	
	Points gained	

GENEROUS PLUTOCRAT

In a town of 1,450 people there lived a rich man. Just before judgement day arrived he wanted to give all of the males in the town a certain sum of money and all of the females in the town $3.00. Of the males, however, only one half claimed the money and of the females only one third claimed the money.

He gave away a total of $1,450. How much did he give each male?

ANSWER:

16.3	Minutes allowed	5
	Time taken	
	Points gained	

WORK THIS ONE OUT!

What is the total value of the symbols in the diagonal from top left to bottom right?

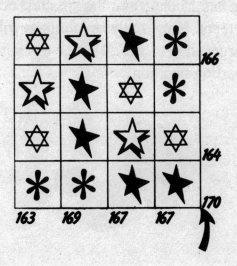

ANSWER:

16.4	Minutes allowed	5
	Time taken	
	Points gained	

COGITATION

Imagine 4 cogs in a constant mesh. The largest cog has 25 teeth, the next cog has 20 teeth, the next cog has 15 teeth and the smallest cog has only 10 teeth. How many revolutions will it take of the largest cog to get all of the other cogs back to the starting position?

ANSWER:

16.5

Minutes allowed	15
Time taken	
Points gained	

SQUARES WITHIN SQUARES

Here is an eight by eight grid. How many squares of any size are there within the diagram?

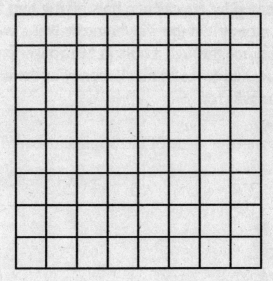

ANSWER:

16.6

Minutes allowed	10
Time taken	
Points gained	

TRANSPOSITION MUDDLES

A man cashed a cheque at the bank and discovered that the pounds and pence has been transposed by the cashier, thus giving him far more money. On the way home he lost a two pence piece through a hole in his trouser pocket. He now had twice as much money as the original cheque was for.

What was the value of the original cheque?

ANSWER:

16.7	Minutes allowed	10
	Time taken	
	Points gained	

IT ALL COMES OUT THE SAME

Look at the diagram below. You have to fill in the missing numbers in such a way that each of the horizontal, vertical and diagonal lines add up to 400. The missing numbers are as follows: 80, 60, 60, 50, 70, 100, 100, 110 and 90.

ANSWER:

16.8

Minutes allowed	10
Time taken	
Points gained	

PARENTHESES

Here are some triangles. All you have to do is replace the brackets in the last triangle with the number that you think should go in their place.

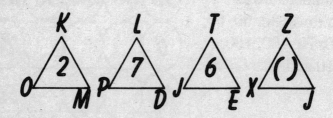

ANSWER:

16.9	Minutes allowed	5
	Time taken	
	Points gained	

TREBLE CROSSING

How many different ways can you find of
constructing a figure out of the diagram below
which comprises three squares with a cross in
and one blank square. By different we mean that
an alternative combination of squares is used,
even though that com-
bination is but one
square different from
the last.

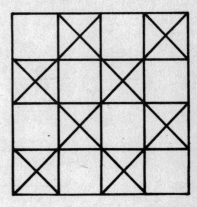

ANSWER:

16.10

Minutes allowed	10
Time taken	
Points gained	

FIT IT IN

How many time will the shape "A" fit into shape "B"? There must be no gaps, and the shapes must be whole and not cut at all.

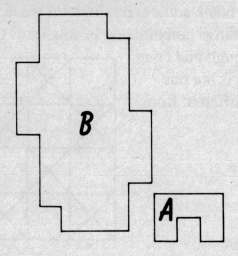

ANSWER:

16.11	Minutes allowed	10
	Time taken	
	Points gained	

MAKE UP YOUR MIND

Here are the letters of the word MIND. You have to work out how many possible ways there are of forming the word from the letters. You can use the same letters in any form of the word. For the sake of this puzzle, every M, I, N and D are treated as being different.

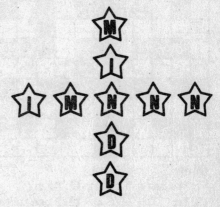

ANSWER:

<table>
<tr><td rowspan="3">16.12</td><td>Minutes allowed</td><td>5</td></tr>
<tr><td>Time taken</td><td></td></tr>
<tr><td>Points gained</td><td></td></tr>
</table>

TIMED CROSSWORD

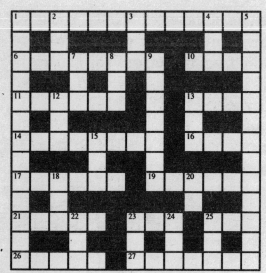

Across

1. Bird (7,6)
6. Writing paper 22" x 30" (8)
10. Projectiles (abbrev) (4)
11. Detain (6)
13. Skating jump (4)
14. Orchestral music (8)
16. Limbs (4)
17. Worship building (6)
19. Sheikh, Saudi Arabian politician (6)
21. American homestead (5)
23. Unit of pressure (3)
25. Garland of flowers (3)
26. Diary account (5)
27. Chambre, peut-etre! (7)

Down

1. Mexican dish (5,3,5)
2. Tear (3)
3. Sea inlet (3)
4. Tree (3)
5. Abstract painting (13)
7. First lady (3)
8. Electrically charged atom (3)
9. Ticket game (7)
12. Often used before a noun (3)
13. Khan (3)
15. Blood sucker (3)
18. Tea container (3)
20. Yours truly (2)
22. Transportation (3)
23. Upper part of an apron (3)
24. Colour (3)
25. Lion (3)

16.13	Minutes allowed	30
	Time taken	
	Points gained	

FIND SIGN – MAKE NINE

Using the following numbers and any mathematical signs you require, can you work out a sum to which the answer is 9?

Here are the numbers: 1, 7, 11 and 14.

ANSWER:

16.14	Minutes allowed	5
	Time taken	
	Points gained	

DIY CROSSWORD

The words down and across are given below, but you must decide where the blank squares are.

I								P
		N						
			A					
	O					R		
E								M

```
STRANDS   ROC    G
EMMET     IBEX   Y
EWER      IRONY  R
STEM      GRIP   A
ACE  BAG  ERA    T
ARE  TEN  R    T E
P    H    I    T D
E    B    A    R
N    R    T    A
T    E    E    C
     S    D    E
```

```
I   I   E   R   M      E   B
T   C   R   O   A      G   A
E   E   E   W   T      O   R
M
```

16.15	Minutes allowed	30
	Time taken	
	Points gained	

ANSWERS

	Your Time	Time Allowed	Points Gained
16.1 Each face of a tetrahedron meets other faces at a linear edge. If you draw a line back from that edge and parallel to it on both faces, those two lines are parallel. The cut which joined them would form a rectangle. If you take the line back far enough they will form a square.		5	

16.2 8 minutes		10	
16.3 £2.00 each		5	
16.4 167		5	
16.5 12 revolutions		15	
16.6 204 squares		10	
16.7 £32.65		10	

CARRIED FORWARD

ANSWERS

FOR CORRECT ANSWERS
Your   Time   Points
Time   Allowed   Gained

BROUGHT FORWARD

	Your Time	Time Allowed	Points Gained
16.8 90 50 130 30 100 0 100 110 90 100 110 100 80 60 50 140 70 50 60 80 60 80 30 160 70			10
16.9 5 (A=1 etc; add top number to bottom left and divide by bottom right			5
16.10 There are 12 ways			10
16.11 8 times			10
16.12 24 times			5
16.13 Across 1. Carrier Pigeon **6.** Imperial **10.** Ammo **11.** Intern **13.** Axel **14.** Overture **16.** Arms **17.** Church **19.** Yamani **21.** Ranch **23.** Bar **25.** Lei **26.** Entry **27.** Bedroom **Down 1.** Chilli con carne **2.** Rip **3.** Ria **4.** Elm **5.** Neoplasticism **7.** Eve **8.** Ion **9.** Lottery **12.** The **13.** Aga **15.** Tic **18.** Urn **20.** Me **22.** Car **23.** Bib **24.** Red **25.** Leo			30

CARRIED FORWARD

ANSWERS

		FOR CORRECT ANSWERS		
		Your Time	Time Allowed	Points Gained
	POINTS BROUGHT FORWARD			
16.14	$(14 \times 7 + 1) \div 11 = 9$		5	
16.15	Answer below		30	
	TOTAL POINTS GAINED			

CHAPTER SUMMARY

Chapter Handicap Total:

Correct Answers x 5 points:

Chapter Total:

   Brought Forward:

   Running Total:

CHAPTER SEVENTEEN

Target Time: 2 hours 55 minutes

MISTAKES ABOUT MISTAKES

"THISS SENTENSE HASS FIVE MISSTAKES"

Is this statement true or false?

ANSWER:

	Minutes allowed	5
17.1	Time taken	
	Points gained	

QUIZ

Answers

1.   Which person invented the automobile in 1885?

2.   Do frogs have teeth?

3.   How many years of bad luck follow breaking a mirror?

4.   What is the most common colour of amethyst?

5.   Which surface is "fine and powdery"?

6.   How many stars are there in Orion's belt?

7.   What did Alan Shephard hit on the moon?

8.   How much thicker than water is blood?

9.   What is a "Citrus grandis"?

10. What is the process for splitting atoms called?

11. What is a crow bar?

12. What is special about the komodo dragon?

17.2	Minutes allowed	**15**
	Time taken	
	Points gained	

GIVEAWAY

In a certain town of 66,000 people there lived a rich man. He offered £38.00 to each male and a certain amount to each female. Of the males, only a nineteenth collected their money, and of all the females only two out of every ten collected their money.

If he gave away £132,000.00 in total, how much did each female receive?

ANSWER:

17.3

Minutes allowed	5
Time taken	
Points gained	

GET RICH QUICK!

A man cashed a cheque at the bank, and discovered that the cashier had transposed the pounds for pence and the pence for pounds, thus giving him more money. He went home on the bus and that cost him 42 pence. He then realised that he had exactly three times the amount of the original cheque.

What was the value of the original cheque?

ANSWER:

17.4	Minutes allowed	5
	Time taken	
	Points gained	

A DOZEN DOZEN SCORE

Imagine a twelve by twelve square. How many rectangles of any size can you construct from it?

It may help you if you draw it out . . .

ANSWER:

17.5	Minutes allowed	15
	Time taken	
	Points gained	

AGAINST THE TIDE

A ship is battling against the tide to safety. Behind it is a waterfall and in front exactly fourteen miles away is an island. The ship is travelling at two miles per hour, but the water is flowing against the ship at one mile every two hours. The ship is using two gallons of fuel every hour, but has only nine gallons left.

Will it reach the safety of the island?

ANSWER:

17.6

Minutes allowed	**10**
Time taken	
Points gained	

INSERT, CREATE

Fill in the missing letters below to create eight words, and a ninth word will be created downwards. What are the nine words?

A ( ) ASH
UP ( ) N
SWO ( ) D
RA ( ) E
BEA ( ) S
CR ( ) AM
OW ( ) ER

ANSWER:

17.7

Minutes allowed	5
Time taken	
Points gained	

NEW LETTERS FOR OLD

Replace the first letter in the words on each side of the brackets with another letter to create two new words. Place this new letter in the brackets and create a seven-letter word downwards. What is it?

PAW ( ) TIGHT
SIGH ( ) SEAT
LAMB ( ) ENTER
SEAL ( ) PASSAGE
PASS ( ) SIX
HAT ( ) GEL
MAT ( ) MULE

ANSWER:

17.8	Minutes allowed	**10**
	Time taken	
	Points gained	

TRANSFORMERS

Change TOIL to FOOD and TEAR to WEEP in as few steps as possible, changing one letter at a time and always creating a new acceptable word.

T O I L	T E A R
· · · ·	· · · ·
· · · ·	· · · ·
· · · ·	· · · ·
· · · ·	· · · ·
F O O D	W E E P

ANSWER:

17.9	Minutes allowed	10
	Time taken	
	Points gained	

LOST PETS

"TO CHARM GETS A BIT DRAB."

From the above sentence can you find four
domestic pets by using all the letters?

ANSWER:

17.10

Minutes allowed	10
Time taken	
Points gained	

WORDPLAY

a) What is the longest word you can find that begins with "A", ends with "Y" and has a connection with order?

b) Which refreshment can be made from the letters of the words "WINTER COAT"?

ANSWER:

17.11	Minutes allowed	15
	Time taken	
	Points gained	

TEN LETTERS

What ten letter word begins with "S", ends with "M", contains another "M" and has a connection with Thorn apples?

ANSWER:

17.12	Minutes allowed	15
	Time taken	
	Points gained	

HOW MANY CAME?

At an exclusive ball the total amount taken on ticket sales was $9,540.00. The attendance was between 70 and 100, and each person paid exactly the same amount in full dollars only.

How much was each ticket and how many people went to the ball?

ANSWER:

17.13	Minutes allowed	15
	Time taken	
	Points gained	

YOU'LL HAVE A FIT

The lettered shapes below can be used to create the larger shapes numbered 1, 2 & 3, as in the example which uses shapes A & B. Which lettered shapes are required to create shapes 1, 2 & 3?

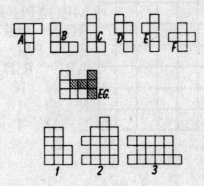

ANSWER:

17.14	Minutes allowed	**10**
	Time taken	
	Points gained	

DIY CROSSWORD

The words down and across are given below, but
you must decide where the blank squares are.

F									
	J				Z				
			Y						
I									S

ACNE ITEM R C
RECTITUDE E R
FORE IMPS C U
MEGAPHONE T C
ROW JAR A I
ZIP PAL N F
ARE RID G O
O N K E L R
R O I A E M
E D T T

W F E I S N
E A W M P I
D R E P Y P
S E R I

17.15

Minutes allowed	30
Time taken	
Points gained	

ANSWERS

| | FOR CORRECT ANSWERS | |
Your Time	Time Allowed	Points Gained

17.1 If your answer is "false" you are wrong, because you have left out the miscount of the number of mistakes. But if your answer is "true" you are wrong because there is no miscount and only four spelling mistakes. This is a classic Russellian paradox. Score 20 points if you noticed the paradox — 5 —

17.2 1. Karl Benz 2. Yes 3. Seven 4. Purple 5. The moon 6. Three 7. A golf ball 8. Six times 9. A grapefruit 10. Fission 11. A jemmy 12. It is the largest living lizard — 15 —

17.3 The women received £10.00 each — 5 —

17.4 The original cheque was for £19.59 — 5 —

17.5 You can construct 6,084 rectangles — 15 —

17.6 The ship will not reach safety — 10 —

CARRIED FORWARD

ANSWERS

FOR CORRECT ANSWERS

	Your Time	Time Allowed	Points Gained

BROUGHT FORWARD

		Time Allowed	
17.7 A (W) ASH UP (O) N SWO (R) D RA (K) E BEA (M) S CRE (A) M OW (N) ER		5	
17.8 Shimmer		10	
17.9 TOIL, TOOL, FOOL, FOOD / TEAR, PEAR, PEER, PEEP, WEEP		10	
17.10 Dog. Cat. Rabbit. Hamster		10	
17.11 **a)** Alphabetically **b)** Tonic water		15	
17.12 Stramonium		15	
17.13 90 people attended and each ticket cost $106		15	
17.14 **1)** C and D **2)** D, E and F **3)** A, D and E		10	
17.15 See answer overleaf			

CARRIED FORWARD

ANSWERS

POINTS BROUGHT FORWARD

17.15 Answer below | 30 |

TOTAL POINTS GAINED

CHAPTER SUMMARY

Chapter Handicap Total:

Correct Answers x 5 points:

Chapter Total:

Brought Forward:

Running Total:

CHAPTER EIGHTEEN

Target Time: 3 hours 5 minutes

ONE CUT HEXAGON

Take a perfect wooden cube. You have to find a
way to saw through it with one straight cut which
divides it equally so as to produce two perfectly
hexagonal surfaces with no messing.

ANSWER:

18.1

Minutes allowed	15
Time taken	
Points gained	

MARK THAT DOPE!

Can you change the word DOPE to MARK in only four steps. You have to change one letter at a time and create a new word at each step.

D O P E

. . . .

. . . .

M A R K

ANSWER:

18.2	Minutes allowed	5
	Time taken	
	Points gained	

FIND THE WATERS

Using all the letters from the following short
sentence can you create four words which have a
connection with inland waterways?

"BEN RETURNED MY ARK"

ANSWER:

18.3	Minutes allowed	15
	Time taken	
	Points gained	

MAKE UP YOUR MIND – AGAIN

The letters in this grid spell the word MIND. How many ways are there of collecting the letters of the word in any order? The rules are that you must always start at the centre letter and then collect four letters. You can then start again but must not retrace your steps. You can only move from a circle to a touching circle.

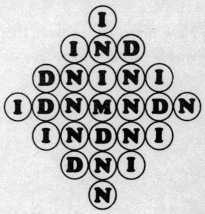

ANSWER:

18.4	Minutes allowed	10
	Time taken	
	Points gained	

WORDS AND PAGES

There was a dictionary containing 60,165 words. It had more than 300 pages but less than 350, and it had less than 235 words on each page. However, there were the same number of words on each page.

How many pages were there, and how many words on each page?

ANSWER:

18.5

Minutes allowed	15
Time taken	
Points gained	

AMAZING SEARCH

Only one of the four entrances will lead the centre of the labyrinth. Which one is it?

ANSWER:

18.6	Minutes allowed	15
	Time taken	
	Points gained	

BAR ARCHERY

The mini-archery target below was designed for use in pubs. It has eight segments, and you have three arrows. The object of the game is to score 120. You can land in any segment any number of times, but you can't reuse combinations of numbers. How many different ways are there of scoring 120?

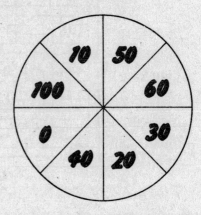

ANSWER:

18.7	Minutes allowed	10
	Time taken	
	Points gained	

A BIG PROBLEM

Below is a plan of the galaxy with four outer planets and nine inner planets. You have to visit one of the outer planets and four of the inner planets, travelling along the thin black lines. The figures represent the number of light years it takes to reach each planet. What is the shortest possible time it would take to visit five planets, starting with one of the outer planets?

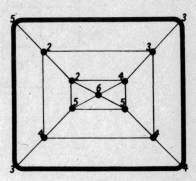

ANSWER:

18.8	Minutes allowed	**10**
	Time taken	
	Points gained	

SQUARE HARVEST

How many squares are there in the diagram below?

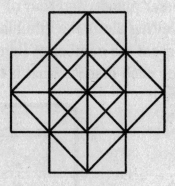

ANSWER:

18.9

Minutes allowed	10
Time taken	
Points gained	

THREE QUICKIES

a) A cup and saucer together way 12 oz. The cup weighs twice as much as the saucer. How much does the saucer weigh?

b) Mary and Jane went shopping for sweets together with 66p between them. Mary started out with 6p more than Jane, but spent twice as much as Jane. Mary ended up with two-thirds as much money as Jane. How much did Jane spend?

c) The hour hand of my clock works perfectly, but the minute hand runs anti-clockwise at a constant speed, crossing the hour hand every 80 minutes. If it was right at 6.30, when will it next show the right time?

ANSWER:

18.10	Minutes allowed	10
	Time taken	
	Points gained	

TRAIN WAYS

The diagram below is a simplified plan of a
railway system, showing lines and points. How
many different ways are there for a train to go
from A to B without reversing?

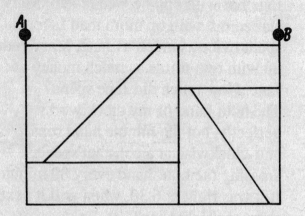

ANSWER:

18.11	Minutes allowed	**10**
	Time taken	
	Points gained	

CHOOSING CHOCS

In the diagram below, each symbol stands for a different type of chocolate packed in a cruciform box. You must start at the centre chocolate and move upwards, downwards or across from square to touching square – but not diagonally – collecting chocolates as you go. How many different ways are there of collecting one of each type of chocolate?

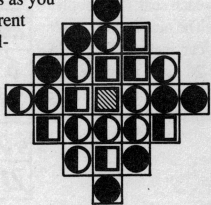

ANSWER:

18.12

Minutes allowed	10
Time taken	
Points gained	

CURIOUS SEATING PLAN

The diagram below represents the seating plan for a public concert. Work on the plan has been started, but you need to finish it. The requirement is that every row, vertically and horizontally, and the two main diagonals, must each seat 120 people. The nine central boxes can include 21, 22, 24, 26 or 27 people each. Can you complete the plan?

26	38	27	2	27
6				35
27				21
40				15
21	7	21	49	22

ANSWER:

18.13

Minutes allowed	10
Time taken	
Points gained	

WHAT AM I?

Can you solve this riddle?

My first is in HALL, but not in ROOM,
My second is in BANG, but not in BOOM,
My third is in WISH, but not in BONE,
My fourth is in FLY, but not in FLOWN,
My fifth is in HOUSE, and also in HOME
To which I return wherever I roam;
To complete the whole, my last is in RUBBLE,
And I'm there to help you, if you are in trouble.

ANSWER:

18.14	Minutes allowed	8
	Time taken	
	Points gained	

DIY CROSSWORD

The words down and across are given below, but you must decide where the blank squares are.

				J			
			S				
			V				
	S						
J							
	V						

STARLET NIL   S
EVENT   BAR   S E
SEA AVERT   S R
STEW   JUMP   R R
CEDE   STAY   A
APE ARE TOR   A T
E   A   P   J   E
L   A   A   A
A   L   T   B
T   E   H   S
E   T   R   E
U   M   S   V   T
U   S   E   R   O   E
S   E   N   A   T   R   E
E   R   A   I   P   O   R
   E   P   T   D   E

18.15

Minutes allowed	30
Time taken	
Points gained	

ANSWERS

	Your Time	Time Allowed	Points Gained
18.1 Your explanation should match the diagram below. If you drew the diagram correctly, take an extra mark.			

	Your Time	Time Allowed	Points Gained
		15	
18.2 DOPE, MOPE, MORE, MARE, MARK		5	
18.3 BUR, MERE, TARN, DYKE		15	
18.4 There are 11 ways of collecting the letters M, I, N and D		10	
18.5 There are 315 pages with 191 words on each		15	
18.6 Entrance B		15	
18.7 You can score 120 nine different ways		10	

CARRIED FORWARD

ANSWERS

FOR CORRECT ANSWERS

	Your Time	Time Allowed	Points Gained

BROUGHT FORWARD

18.8 14 light years — 10

18.9 There are a total of 27 squares in the diagram — 10

18.10 a) 4 oz
b) 12 pence
c) At 7.06 — 10

18.11 There are 16 different routes from A to B — 10

18.12 There are 10 different ways of selecting four different chocolates — 10

18.13

26	38	27	2	27
6	27	26	26	35
27	26	24	22	21
40	22	22	21	15
21	7	21	49	22

10

18.14 LAWYER — 8

18.15 See answer overleaf

CARRIED FORWARD

ANSWERS

FOR CORRECT ANSWERS

	Your Time	Time Allowed	Points Gained
POINTS BROUGHT FORWARD			
18.15 Answer below		30	
TOTAL POINTS GAINED			

S	T	A	Y		J	U	M	P
N	I	L		S		S	E	A
A	P	E		E	V	E	N	T
P		R		R				H
	S	T	A	R	L	E	T	
J			A		L			M
A	V	E	R	T		A	R	E
B	A	R		E		T	O	R
S	T	E	W		C	E	D	E

CHAPTER SUMMARY

Chapter Handicap Total:

Correct Answers x 5 points:

Chapter Total:

Brought Forward:

Running Total:

CHAPTER
NINETEEN

Target Time: 2 hours 55 minutes

UNEARTHLY PING PONG

You are the observer of two very heavy projectiles A and B which have, attached in front, large flat sheets of elasticium – the little known metal which is perfectly elastic. The projectiles are on opposite straight paths on a collision course, at a speed relative to you of 100 km per second. A small perfect ball of elasticium is shot from A to B at a speed of 100 km per second, and bounces back and forth between them three complete times before they collide.

At what speed relative to you was the ball moving after its last bounce?

ANSWER:

19.1	Minutes allowed	10
	Time taken	
	Points gained	

GO FORTH AND MULTIPLY

Multiply all the numbers from negative six to positive six, in increments of one, inclusive. What is the result?

-6 x -5 x -4 . . . . 4 x 5 x 6

ANSWER:

19.2	Minutes allowed	5
	Time taken	
	Points gained	

ASTEROIDING

On your way between two planets you encounter an asteroid field, shown below. The figures in each open circle are the number of years taken for that part of your journey. Each black circle represents an asteroid and adds 7 years to your journey. You have to travel from A to B,

following the arrows. How many different routes are there for which the total journey time will be 57 years?

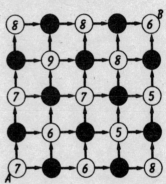

ANSWER:

19.3

Minutes allowed	**10**
Time taken	
Points gained	

LOGICAL TRIANGLES

What should replace the question mark in the last of these four triangles?

ANSWER:

19.4	Minutes allowed	**10**
	Time taken	
	Points gained	

PLANETARY LINE-UP

Here is a map of a planetary system. All three planets revolve around the sun in a clockwise direction. The outer planet takes 16 years to make one revolution; the middle planet takes 12 years and the inner planet takes 4 years. They are now in line with the sun and with each other. When, in full years, will this next occur?

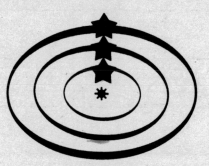

ANSWER:

19.5	Minutes allowed	10
	Time taken	
	Points gained	

CAN YOU COUNT?

How many squares of any size can be counted in this grid?

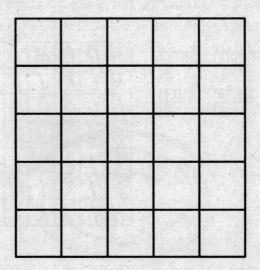

ANSWER:

19.6	Minutes allowed	5
	Time taken	
	Points gained	

LOGICRACKER

Crack the logic and tell us which of the tiles below fits into the gap in the large diagram.

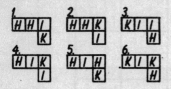

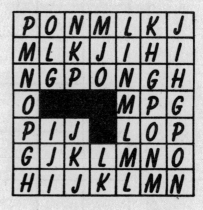

ANSWER:

	19.7	Minutes allowed	10
		Time taken	
		Points gained	

VE HAF VAYS!

How many different routes are there from A to B

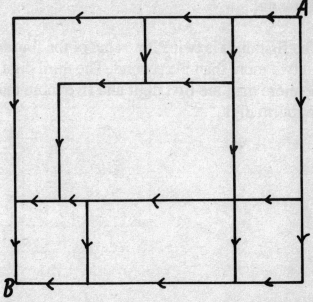

ANSWER:

19.8	Minutes allowed	5
	Time taken	
	Points gained	

FINGER THE DIGITS

Which four-digit number can be described by the following:

"The first digit is twice the value of the fourth and two more than the second. The third digit is one more than the first digit and five more than the fourth digit."

ANSWER:

19.9	Minutes allowed	10
	Time taken	
	Points gained	

CAN YOU MAKE IT?

Which of the six cubes below cannot be made
from the flattened out shape?

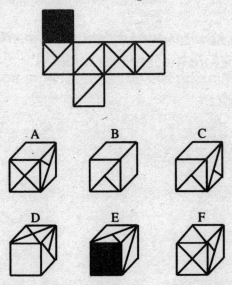

ANSWER:

19.10	Minutes allowed	10
	Time taken	
	Points gained	

WATCH OUT!

Your watch is broken. Every time the second hand passes the '4' it jumps back 12 seconds.

If the time now reads midnight, how many hours will pass before it next reads midday?

ANSWER:

19.11

Minutes allowed	10
Time taken	
Points gained	

QUIZ

1. What kind of cow produces more than 80% of the UK's milk?

2. When would you see Bailey's Beads?

3. What colour is a Granny Smith?

4. Where are a snail's reproductive organs?

5. What was the name of Charles Darwin's ship?

6. How many points are there on a Maltese cross?

7. What puts bubbles in soda water?

8. What makes up 12 per cent of the weight of an egg?

9. Name the smallest bird in the world?

10. Where are the Haversian canals?

11. Who invented the machine gun in 1862?

12. What is the name of the jet engine that powers Concorde?

19.12	Minutes allowed	15
	Time taken	
	Points gained	

UNJUMBLE

The following six groups of letters are words that have been jumbled up. What are the words?

a)   BROUNTHEAD

b)   GATESTILEUC

c)   HIARQULEN

d)   BROKENKICKERC

e)   EVERPICSHIRE

f)   CREATEFOODNIN

ANSWER:

19.13	Minutes allowed	20
	Time taken	
	Points gained	

NUMBER TRACKS

You have to start at one of the corner numbers
and follow the thin lines to collect four other
numbers. You then add all five numbers together
to give you a total for that route. How many
different ways are there of collecting a total of
33? You can't "back
track" or use the
same route twice
in any way.

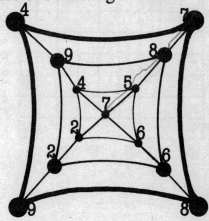

ANSWER:

DIY CROSSWORD

The words down and across are given below, but you must decide where the blank squares are.

O								S
				C				
G								
				R				
								R
				E				
A								W

INTRUDE OFT
DEBAR OYEZ
AXLE GULCH
BOSS ANEW
VAT VIA ICE
ROE ODE

CHARADE
STEM DREW ORGY VOID NATAL

NOVA YOU SAD FIX BIN ACE EEL

19.15	Minutes allowed	30
	Time taken	
	Points gained	

ANSWERS

| | | FOR CORRECT ANSWERS | | |
		Your Time	Time Allowed	Points Gained
19.1	The answer may surprise. It is 800 km/s. Relative to you, the observer, at the first pass it meets B at 200 km/s, its speed plus the projectile's speed. But the mutual velocity is 300 km/s. It bounces back from B to A at that speed plus that of the surface of B which it bounced off, making 400 km/s. It hits A at 500 km/s, plus the speed of A makes 600 km/s. The next mutual speed is 700 km/s and final speed relative to you is 800 km/s		10	
19.2	Zero (one of the numbers is 0)		5	
19.3	There are 8 routes		10	
19.4	5 (the total of each like positioned number is 25)		10	
19.5	24 years		10	
19.6	55 squares		5	
19.7	The missing shape is number 5		10	

CARRIED FORWARD

ANSWERS

FOR CORRECT ANSWERS
Your   Time   Points
Time   Allowed   Gained

BROUGHT FORWARD

		Your Time	Time Allowed	Points Gained
19.8	10 routes		5	
19.9	8,694		10	
19.10	B, E and F		10	
19.11	It will never reach midday unless it is mended		10	
19.12	1. Friesian 2. During a total solar eclipse 3. It's a green apple 4. Its head 5. The Beagle 6. Eight 7. Carbon dioxide 8. The shell 9. Hummingbird 10. In the bones 11. J. R. Gatling 12. Olympus		15	
19.13	a) Earthbound b) Gesticulate c) Harlequin d) Knickerbocker e) Receivership f) Confederation		20	
19.14	There are 9 ways		15	
19.15	See answer overleaf			

CARRIED FORWARD

366

ANSWERS

FOR CORRECT ANSWERS

	Your Time	Time Allowed	Points Gained

POINTS BROUGHT FORWARD

19.15   Answer below

		30	

TOTAL POINTS GAINED

```
O Y E Z   B O S S
R O E   C   V A T
G U L C H   O D E
Y       A   I   M
  I N T R U D E
N   A   A     D
O F T   D E B A R
V I A   E   I C E
A X L E   A N E W
```

CHAPTER SUMMARY

Chapter Handicap Total:

Correct Answers x 5 points:

Chapter Total:

Brought Forward:

Running Total:

CHAPTER TWENTY

Target Time: 2 hours 22 minutes

CONTRA WALKING 1

On a train or a plane you can walk south when you are moving north, but how can you contra walk when your own walking is all that affects your motion relative to the surface? You walk forwards but you go backwards. How come?

ANSWER:

20.1	Minutes allowed	5
	Time taken	
	Points gained	

CONTRA WALKING 2

A pedestrian walks three miles due south. She ten stops. Next she walks three miles due north. She has walked six miles and she is six miles away from where she started, instead of being back there. How come?

There are many places she might have been. How would you map them?

ANSWER:

	Minutes allowed	5
20.2	Time taken	
	Points gained	

BALL GAME

Can you convert BALL into GAME in only three steps? You must change one letter at each step, and with the change a good, new English word must be formed.

B A L L

. . . .

. . . .

G A M E

ANSWER:

20.3	Minutes allowed	5
	Time taken	
	Points gained	

GOAL POST

Convert GOAL into POST in four steps, changing one letter at a time and forming an acceptable English word at each step.

G O A L

. . . .

. . . .

. . . .

P O S T

ANSWER:

20.4	Minutes allowed	5
	Time taken	
	Points gained	

LETTER TO SIGN

The top two calculations work when the same mathematical sign is placed in the position of like letters (eg, if you think "A" in the first calculation means multiply, it must mean the same in the second calculation). Once you have worked out what "A", "B" and "C" represent, apply them to the third calculation and work out the number which should replace the "?".

9 A 3 B 6 C 9 = 9

8 A 4 B 3 C 2 = 4

? A 6 B 9 C 4 = 5

ANSWER:

20.5	Minutes allowed	4
	Time taken	
	Points gained	

THE LOST CONSONANTS

Here is a quotation uttered at the New York Custom House. All of the consonants have been replaced by diamonds, but the vowels remain. What is the quote, and who said it?

"I ◊A◊E ◊O◊◊I◊◊ ◊O ◊E◊◊A◊E E◊◊E◊◊ ◊Y ◊E◊IU◊"

ANSWER:

20.6	Minutes allowed	3
	Time taken	
	Points gained	

DOUBLE CHALLENGE

a) On what day of the week did January 1772 fall?

b) Which two words, that use the same six letters, can be placed in the spaces in this sentence to make the most sense?

"Blackbeard the evil pirate always . . . . . . his treasure since one day he kept the . . . . . ., because he liked the colour, and was stopped at the customs and made to pay duty."

ANSWER:

20.7	Minutes allowed	25
	Time taken	
	Points gained	

FUSSY SALLY

Sally likes khaki, but not brown. She likes pyjamas, but not nightgowns. She likes chocolate mousse, but not bread pudding. Will she like slacks or jodhpurs?

ANSWER:

	Minutes allowed	5
20.8	Time taken	
	Points gained	

PHRASE MUDDLE

The following letters can be rearranged to spell five words that refer to an event which is compared to a large mammal. Here are the letters, what is the phrase?

EEAAAWTOMFHIL

ANSWER:

20.9

Minutes allowed	10
Time taken	
Points gained	

CONFUSED ASSIGNATION

A gentleman says to his fair lady, "We will meet three days after the day before the day before tomorrow."

If today is Monday, when will they meet?

ANSWER:

20.10	Minutes allowed	5
	Time taken	
	Points gained	

WORD SQUARE

A word square is composed of words that read across and down. Here are four definitions. If you fill in the words correctly, you will create a word square.

1) Small path or narrow road
2) A space covered, a geometry term
3) In close proximity
4) All animals have them

ANSWER:

20.11

Minutes allowed	10
Time taken	
Points gained	

AND ANOTHER

Here is another word square. Solve the clues and complete it.

1) A musical notation

2) Not under

3) Rip

4) It's human when done

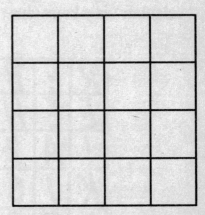

ANSWER:

20.12	Minutes allowed	10
	Time taken	
	Points gained	

ANOTHER LOGICRACKER

Crack the logic and calculate which letter should replace the question mark. By the way, "calculate" is a huge clue!

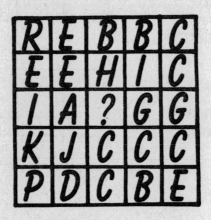

ANSWER:

20.13	Minutes allowed	**10**
	Time taken	
	Points gained	

ALWAYS ANOTHER WAY

Here is an eight-segment dart board, and you have three darts. You have to calculate how many different ways there are of scoring 20 with three darts. Once a combination has been used it can be reused in a different order, as many times as possible. So, how many ways are there of scoring 20?

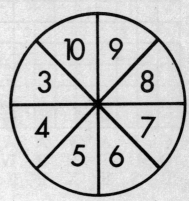

ANSWER:

20.14

Minutes allowed	10
Time taken	
Points gained	

DIY CROSSWORD

The words down and across are given below, but you must decide where the blank squares are.

			X					
	U						W	
		Y					Y	
	V							
	X							W

MYSTERY USE
VET BAR RUM
APEX STEW
REBEL OWE
ORE OVALS
SCAB AXED

PROTEST
ROBOT
BELL ARUM NOVA BREW
EMERY
COB PUS ATE VEX ARE AWE

20.15	Minutes allowed	30
	Time taken	
	Points gained	

ANSWERS

	Your Time	Time Allowed	Points Gained
20.1 You are walking on top of a ball or drum on land, or a log in the water		5	

20.2 She was anywhere on a circle 3 miles from the south pole. When she reached the pole she did not turn, she just kept going in a straight line		5	
20.3 BALL, GALL (or BALE), GALE, GAME		5	
20.4 GOAL, GOAT, MOAT, MOST, POST		5	
20.5 The missing figure is 6 $A = +$, $B = \times$, $C = -$		4	

CARRIED FORWARD

ANSWERS

	FOR CORRECT ANSWERS		
	Your Time	Time Allowed	Points Gained
BROUGHT FORWARD			
20.6 "I have nothing to declare except my own genius." Uttered by Oscar Wilde		3	
20.7 a) Monday. It was a leap year b) BURIES & RUBIES		25	
20.8 Jodhpurs. She likes words of foreign origin		5	
20.9 A whale of a time		10	
20.10 Wednesday		5	
20.11 L A N E A R E A N E A R E A R S		10	
20.12 N O T E O V E R T E A R E R R S		10	
20.13 F (A = 15, B = 16 etc and each row = 100)		10	
20.14 48 ways		10	
20.15 See answer overleaf			
CARRIED FORWARD			

ANSWERS

FOR CORRECT ANSWERS

	Your Time	Time Allowed	Points Gained

POINTS BROUGHT FORWARD

20.15 Answer below | | 30 |

TOTAL POINTS GAINED

```
A P E X   S C A B
R U M   P   O W E
U S E   R E B E L
M   R   O       L
  M Y S T E R Y
N       E   O   B
O V A L S   B A R
V E T   T   O R E
A X E D   S T E W
```

CHAPTER SUMMARY

Chapter Handicap Total:

Correct Answers x 5 points:

Chapter Total:

Brought Forward:

Running Total:

CHAPTER
TWENTY ONE

Target Time: 3 hours 30 minutes

A HYDRA OBJECT

I have in my hand a solid object called a 'squiffle', which reminds me of the Hydra – the nine-headed monster that Hercules came up against. This squiffle has four things on it – let us call them 'driggles'. If I cut off these four driggles with my knife, I discover that my squiffle now has twelve driggles. In fact, it is no longer a squiffle, but the four driggles which I cut off have transformed themselves into squiffles! And since each of these has four driggles, I now have a total of 28 driggles.

What is a squiffle, and what is a driggle? They both have other names.

ANSWER:

21.1	Minutes allowed	15
	Time taken	
	Points gained	

WORD CHAIN

By changing one letter at a time to create a different word, what is the least number of steps needed to change the word CILL to BAIT?

ANSWER:

	Minutes allowed	5
21.2	Time taken	
	Points gained	

SCORE? YOU NAME IT!

A number of friends at school sat a test, and they all scored terribly. Each score is a percentage, and for some reason it is connected with the student's name. Crack the logic and calculate the score which Ann achieved.

SIDNEY	20
MALCOLM	22
JEAN	16
PHOEBE	24
ANN	?

ANSWER:

21.3

Minutes allowed	8
Time taken	
Points gained	

HAVE A FIT

Which of the shapes 1 to 5 should be placed into the empty space in the grid below?

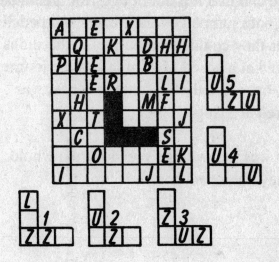

ANSWER:

21.4	Minutes allowed	12
	Time taken	
	Points gained	

SPEED THOSE EGGS

Martin and Matthew Harris were asked to pop to the shops for their parents, who run a Guest House and had run out of eggs for breakfast. They both jumped on their bikes and pedalled as fast as they could. The journey to the shops was covered at a speed of 28mph and the journey back, over exactly the same distance, was covered at 31mph.

What was the average speed for the whole journey, there and back?

ANSWER:

21.5

Minutes allowed	15
Time taken	
Points gained	

LIZ TRACK 3

Starting at the bottom left hand letter work your way either upwards or to the right from square to touching square in such a way that you pass over all of the letters of the name ELIZABETH. To be called a touching square, it must touch along a full edge, not just a corner. How many ways are there of "collecting" all the letters of the name Elizabeth?

A	B	E	T	H
Z	A	E	A	T
I	B	H	B	E
L	I	Z	A	B
E	L	I	Z	A

ANSWER:

21.6	Minutes allowed	10
	Time taken	
	Points gained	

ECLIPSE TIME?

Two planets are in orbit around a sun, as shown in the diagram. At this moment in time they are in line with the sun and are travelling in the direction shown at different speeds. Planet A completes one orbit every 54 years and planet B does the same task every 66 years. When will the two planets and the sun next be in line with each other?

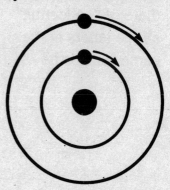

ANSWER:

21.7

Minutes allowed	15
Time taken	
Points gained	

KEEP YOUR BALANCE

The top two sets of scales are in perfect balance. How many of the missing item are needed to balance the third set of scales?

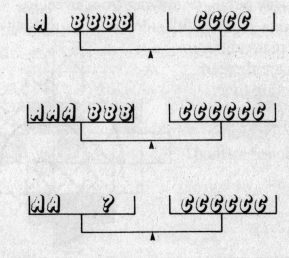

ANSWER:

21.8	Minutes allowed	10
	Time taken	
	Points gained	

ALL SORTS

There are four different types of sweet in this box and, of course, you want one of each. You must always start at the centre sweet and work your way outwards moving from sweet to touching sweet (a full side must be touching). How many different ways are there of collecting four different sweets using the afore-mentioned method?

ANSWER:

21.9	Minutes allowed	8
	Time taken	
	Points gained	

WORD TIDY

What four words can be made from these letters?

a) **MEETTHEMORR**

b) **RATNATACIC**

c) **NONINLATEARTE**

d) **TOJEPERILC**

ANSWER:

21.10	Minutes allowed	12
	Time taken	
	Points gained	

WAYS THROUGH TOWN

Here is a map of a one way system in a town. You are at "A" and, of course, want to be at "B". How many legal ways are there of getting from "A" to "B"?

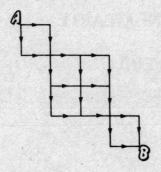

ANSWER:

21.11	Minutes allowed	15
	Time taken	
	Points gained	

COUNTING AROUND

How many different circles are there in this diagram? Colouring a few in might help you!

ANSWER:

21.12

Minutes allowed	15
Time taken	
Points gained	

WHEN A DECADE DECAYED

This is an easy puzzle, especially on a Sunday!
What number should replace the question mark?

7	14	21	
28	4	11	
18	25	4	
11	18	25	?

ANSWER:

21.13	Minutes allowed	**20**
	Time taken	
	Points gained	

A PARTIAL MAGIC CUBE

A magic cube is one where the numbers add up to the same number down, across and through. They are not easy to draw, so I have taken this one apart into three separate layers of nine cells each. I have left some of the numbers out, and it is your job to fill them.

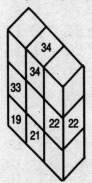
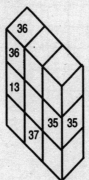
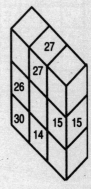

ANSWER:

21.14	Minutes allowed	20
	Time taken	
	Points gained	

DIY CROSSWORD

The words down and across are given below, but you must decide where the blank squares are.

			T			G
	K					
V		.				
		E		D		

SCENE	SKI	G	D
DISSENTER		R	R
LLANO	IRK	E	I
DIPHTHONG		N	V
ELSE	DATA	A	E
APES	ELSE	D	L
P	L	A	C	I	L
O	E	S	C	E	L
K	A	S	E	R	E
E	N	S	D		D
E		E	E		
S		T		T	P
	O	A		T	O
	N	S		O	P
	E	S		S	L

SCENE   SKI   G   D
DISSENTER   R   R
LLANO   IRK   E   I
DIPHTHONG   N   V
ELSE   DATA   A   E
APES   ELSE   D   L
P   L   A   C   I   L
O   E   S   E   E   L
K   A   S   D   R   E
E   N   E   E   D
S   T   T   P
         O   A   O   O
         N   S   S   P
         E   S   S   L
                               E

21.15	Minutes allowed	30
	Time taken	
	Points gained	

ANSWERS

	FOR CORRECT ANSWERS		
	Your Time	Time Allowed	Points Gained

21.1 A squiffle is a four-sided pyramid or tetrahedron. It has four corners, vertices or driggles as I call them. Each cut vertex forms another tetrahedron, which has four vertices or driggles. The original squiffle becomes an octohedron with 12 vertices, while the four new tetrahedra each have four. — 15

21.2 4. CILL CALL BALL BAIL BAIT — 5

21.3 10. Number of vowels x 6 + number of consonants x 4 — 8

21.4 Shape 5. A = 1, B = 2, etc. Each vertical column has a total of 50 — 12

21.5 29.424 mph — 15

21.6 11 ways — 10

21.7 148 years and 6 months. They will be on opposite sides of the sun — 15

21.8 5 Bs. A = 8, B = 4, C = 6 — 10

CARRIED FORWARD

ANSWERS

FOR CORRECT ANSWERS

| | Your Time | Time Allowed | Points Gained |

BROUGHT FORWARD

		Time Allowed	
21.9	There are 11 ways of collecting 4 different sweets	8	
21.10	a) THERMOMETER b) ANTARCTICA c) INTERNATIONAL d) PROJECTILE	12	
21.11	There are 24 routes from "A" to "B"	15	
21.12	There are 17 circles	15	
21.13	1. They are the dates of Sundays at the start of a year such as 1990	20	

21.14

20

21.15 See answer overleaf

CARRIED FORWARD

ANSWERS

Your Time	Time Allowed	Points Gained

POINTS BROUGHT FORWARD

21.15 Answer below | | 30

TOTAL POINTS GAINED

```
D I P H T H O N G
R   O     O   N     R
R I R K     S C E N E
V   E L S E         N
E A S E     D A T A
L     A P E S   D
L L A N O     S K I
E     S   L   E   E
D I S S E N T E R
```

CHAPTER SUMMARY

Chapter Handicap Total:

Correct Answers x 5 points:

Chapter Total:

Brought Forward:

Running Total:

CHAPTER TWENTY TWO

Target Time: 3 hours 55 minutes

EXACT TIME LINE UP

At what time, exactly, between three and four o'clock is the minute hand on a normal clock exactly aligned over the hour hand?

ANSWER:

22.1	Minutes allowed	20
	Time taken	
	Points gained	

GEOMETRICAL SERIES

This is a series. You will find what comes next from what is given. SPHERE. CIRCLE. LINE.

What comes next?

ANSWER:

22.2	Minutes allowed	5
	Time taken	
	Points gained	

FIND THE LETTER

Which letter should replace the question mark in the grid below?

ANSWER:

22.3	Minutes allowed	5
	Time taken	
	Points gained	

MORE COGITATION

Four cogs are in constant mesh, as shown in this diagram. The largest cog has 25 teeth; the next cog, cog B, has 20 teeth; cog C has 15 teeth and the smallest cog has only 10 teeth. How many revolutions will the largest cog have to make before all the cogs return to their original position?

ANSWER:

22.4

Minutes allowed	10
Time taken	
Points gained	

IRRELEVANT COSTING

The travel agent has got some special offers on again, but has not yet written in the price for Germany. Following the same grammatical logic as for the other four, what is the cost of a holiday in Germany?

CORFU	£36
PORTUGAL	£90
TURKEY	£48
GREECE	£54
GERMANY	£ ?

ANSWER:

22.5	Minutes allowed	20
	Time taken	
	Points gained	

LETTER SEARCH

Each letter has a value ranging from one to twenty-six inclusive. Which letter should replace the question mark?

$$O \div U + I = N$$

$$H \div S + A = \;?$$

ANSWER:

22.6	Minutes allowed	20
	Time taken	
	Points gained	

ANOTHER USELESS CLOCK

Your clock has gone haywire. At 2.41 am it read 6.17, at 6.17 it read 9.53, whilst at 9.53 it read 1.29 pm.

What time will it read at 1.29 pm?

ANSWER:

22.7	Minutes allowed	15
	Time taken	
	Points gained	

LOGICAL LETTER?

Following the same logic as for the first three triangles, which letter should replace the question mark in the fourth triangle? It might take days to do this one!

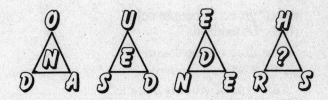

ANSWER:

22.8	Minutes allowed	10
	Time taken	
	Points gained	

QUIZ

1. What do dilute acetic acid and vegetable oil make?

2. What mammal lays eggs, has webbed feet with claws and has a bill?

3. What letter is at the left hand end of the bottom row of a typewriter keyboard?

4. What group of people celebrate Eisteddfods?

5. What drug can be found in tonic water?

6. What type of wool is obtained from angora goats?

7. What is the day before Ash Wednesday?

8. Who discovered Saturn's rings?

9. How many legs does an oyster catcher have?

10. In which month does the harvest moon shine?

11. How many feet in a fathom?

12. What is a third molar called?

22.9	Minutes allowed	15
	Time taken	
	Points gained	

DIY CROSSWORD

The words down and across are given below, but you must decide where the blank squares are.

S					S
	A			I	
		E	I		
		L			
	G			L	
D					L

DEWY LOSS G
NEMESIS ILL A
SPAN MALL Z
EGO LEVEE E
OPERA KIT L
TAR LAD ATE L
O E B B E
K N E L
A D L E
P O L D
I W S S
R I L T T
E I L E O
T A L M W
E P

A S A P V E
R I G A I L
E T E P A L

Minutes allowed		30

22.10

Time taken	
Points gained	

EXTEND THIS STRING

Here is a string of integers. The arrangement is logical. Replace the question marks at each end with the correct figure.

? 18 20 21 22 24 25 26 27 28 ?

ANSWER:

22.11	Minutes allowed	5
	Time taken	
	Points gained	

GRID FILLING

Using only the numbers given below, complete the grid in such a way thay each vertical and horizontal line totals 28.

1 1 2 2 3 4 4 5 5 5 6 7 8 8 8 8 9 9 9

9	4	7	6	2

ANSWER:

22.12	Minutes allowed **15**
	Time taken
	Points gained

DIY CROSSWORD

The words down and across are given below, but you must decide where the blank squares are.

		O		I			
L							T
			A				
C							L
		S		A			

AGES ICON   P
RELAPSE SEX   Y
OLIO WEDS   R
ISSUE VIM   A
ACE APPLY   M
ASS RID ARE   I
C   E   L   O D
A   N   E   V
S   D   S   A
E   E   S   L
S   D   C   N
          R   E
          A   X
          W   T

O L I I S U
R I M C A S
E P P E G E

22.13	Minutes allowed	**30**
	Time taken	
	Points gained	

422

NUMBER TRACKS

Starting at one of the corner numbers, make your way, but following the thin black lines, around the diagram in order to "land" on four other numbers. Add the five figures together, and you have the total for the particular route you have taken. How many different routes are there with a total of 42?

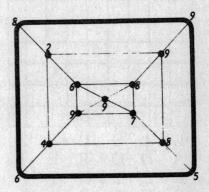

ANSWER:

22.14

Minutes allowed	5
Time taken	
Points gained	

DIY CROSSWORD

The words down and across are given below, but you must decide where the blank squares are.

				J				
		O						
				Z				
		C				A		
					M			

MERE IDOL D P
DECLINATE E R
ELLS SEPT S O
OAR LEA I S
PROCESSED G A
ERA TON N I
AGE GAY A C
O E T E T A
R A O E E L
E R R L

L I S D J Z
A D O E E I
D L P N T P
E E S E

22.15	Minutes allowed	30
	Time taken	
	Points gained	

ANSWERS

	Your Time	Time Allowed	Points Gained

22.1 To be exact we use a rational number rather than a decimal. The exact answer is 16 minutes 21⁴/₁₁ seconds past three. This is the only correct answer. I said exactly, not to the nearest second or even decimal point.   20

22.2 A point. A sphere has 3 dimensions, a circle two, and a line one. A point has no dimensions, only position.   5

22.3 B. Multiply the "coordinates" and using A = 1, or 27, or 53 etc you can work out the letter in each square.   5

22.4 12 revolutions   10

22.5 £60. Multiply twice the vowels by three times the consonants.   20

22.6 G. A = 11, B =12, P = 26, Q = 1 etc.   20

22.7 5.05 p.m. The clock is 3hrs 36 mins fast.   15

CARRIED FORWARD

ANSWERS

BROUGHT FORWARD

22.8 U. Each triangle shows the 2nd to 5th letters of Monday to Thursday. — 10

22.9 **1.** French dressing **2.** The duckbilled platypus **3.** Z **4.** Druids **5.** Quinine **6.** Mohair **7.** Shrov Tuesday **8.** Galileo **9.** 2 **10.** September **11.** Six **12.** A wisdom tooth — 15

22.10

S	P	A	N		L	O	S	S
T	A	R		G		K	I	T
O	P	E	R	A		A	T	E
W				Z		P		M
	N	E	M	E	S	I	S	
B		N		L				B
L	A	D		L	E	V	E	E
E	G	O		E		I	L	L
D	E	W	Y		M	A	L	L

— 30

22.11 16 and 30. The numbers are the non-primes, starting from 16. — 5

CARRIED FORWARD

ANSWERS

FOR CORRECT ANSWERS

	Your Time	Time Allowed	Points Gained

BROUGHT FORWARD

22.12
```
9 4 7 6 2
1 5 6 8 8
8 9 8 1 2
5 2 3 9 9
5 8 4 4 7
```
15

22.13

O	L	I	O		I	C	O	N
V	I	M		P		A	R	E
A	P	P	L	Y		S	E	X
L			R		E		T
	R	E	L	A	P	S	E	
C		N		M				L
R	I	D		I	S	S	U	E
A	C	E		D		A	S	S
W	E	D	S		A	G	E	S

30

22.14 There are 5 routes by which you can score a total of 42 points

5

22.15 See answer overleaf

CARRIED FORWARD

ANSWERS

FOR CORRECT ANSWERS

| Your Time | Time Allowed | Points Gained |

POINTS BROUGHT FORWARD

21.15 Answer below | | 30 |

TOTAL POINTS GAINED

CHAPTER SUMMARY

Chapter Handicap Total:

Correct Answers x 5 points:

Chapter Total:

Brought Forward:

Running Total:

CHAPTER
TWENTY THREE

Target Time: 4 hours 0 minutes

INVISIBLE MAGNETS

You are blindfolded and naked in an empty room. You are given a pair of steel bars. One is a bar magnet, the other is not. You will be released if you can tell which is which. You are allowed to touch them together just once.

How can you tell which is the magnet?

ANSWER:

23.1	Minutes allowed	10
	Time taken	
	Points gained	

HOW TO CHEAT

You are on a holiday tour and the hotel manager is giving a free holiday as a prize. As you go to the final party the guests put their door keys into a bowl so as to draw the winner. The bowl turns out to be too small, and another is added. The manager will toss a coin to decide the winning bowl and then pick the winner from that.

How can you use this to increase your chance?

ANSWER:

23.2	Minutes allowed	5
	Time taken	
	Points gained	

DIY CROSSWORD

The words down and across are given below, but you must decide where the blank squares are.

			K						
		N				T			
								Y	
		X							
	V								

REVERSING	C	A
PATE BADE	O	S
LACK ASPS	N	T
VENERATED	S	E
DIE AGO	E	R
SOD PRY	R	O
VEX ARE	V	I
A A T N	E	D
G R O I P	D	S
O C E P		

C	L	A	E	F	E
R	A	G	D	R	R
A	V	E	D	Y	A
B	A	S	Y		

	23.3	Minutes allowed	30
		Time taken	
		Points gained	

432

GOBS, KALS, ET AL

The fourth planet of Centaur Major is called Grost. The vital taxonomy is much like ours. It is known that all prits are kals, and there are no kals that are not gobs. However, although some zloms may be brups as well as prits, many of both species are not even gobs. Further, all the brups that are zloms are also prits. The problem is simple. Can there be such a weird creature that it falls into all five classes? While being a certified prit, it is also a kal, a gob, a zlom and a brup? Further, can there be creatures on Grost that fall into only one of these classes and, if so, which is it?

ANSWER:

Minutes allowed	15
Time taken	
Points gained	

23.4

CLOCK PATIENCE

I am patient and lazy. I have two clocks which are telling me the correct time, which is twelve o'clock. But one gains five minutes every hour and the other loses five minutes every hour. I could go to the bother of correcting them but I am too idle. I am patient enough just to wait for them to come into agreement of their own accord.

But how long will it take? And will they be right when they do agree?

ANSWER:

23.5	Minutes allowed	15
	Time taken	
	Points gained	

STRANGE SERIES

Give the next number in this series:

22   20   10   8   4   2   ?

ANSWER:

23.6

Minutes allowed	10
Time taken	
Points gained	

THREE-LETTER WORD

There are three numbers which in a sense are progressive. The product in terms of the second – of the first to the power of the sum of the first and the third, the second to the power of itself and the third to the power of the first – can be expressed as a three-letter everday word.

What, I pray, may be that word?

ANSWER:

23.7

Minutes allowed	20
Time taken	
Points gained	

CONTROLLED BREEDING

A dictator of a polygamous country wanted more girls to be born because every man wanted several wives. The wives in the harems were allowed to have children until the first boy, so there could be no more than one boy per family. He envisaged families with plenty of girls but only one boy each.

What would happen if the scheme worked? Would it result in a greater proportion of girls? If not, what was the flaw in the logic? What would be the result of such a foolish and inhuman rule?

ANSWER:

23.8	Minutes allowed	15
	Time taken	
	Points gained	

ALIEN MAGIC SQUARE

Here is a suspected magic square (all rows, columns and diagonals sum to a constant). It was found inside a meteorite. It is the only way we have of deciphering the number system employed by the aliens who sent it. We do not know the base, the meaning of the symbols, or the way of indicating the order of base units. What is the base? Can you fill in the magic square?

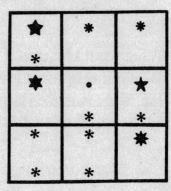

ANSWER:

23.9	Minutes allowed	20
	Time taken	
	Points gained	

DIY CROSSWORD

The words down and across are given below, but you must decide where the blank squares are.

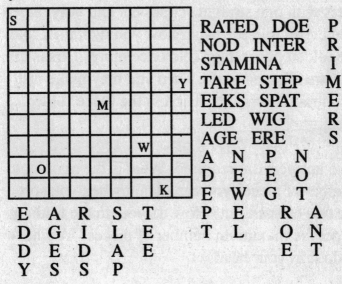

RATED   DOE   P
NOD   INTER   R
STAMINA   I
TARE   STEP   M
ELKS   SPAT   E
LED   WIG   R
AGE   ERE   S
A   N   P   N
D   E   E   O
E   W   G   T
P   E   R   A
T   L   O   N
      E   T

E   A   R   S   T
D   G   I   L   E
D   E   D   A   E
Y   S   S   P

23.10	Minutes allowed	30
	Time taken	
	Points gained	

MAXIMISING MESS

Imagine this. You take a piece of writing paper. Your task is to make the maximum amount of mess with one straight scissor cut and only three folds. You fold the paper how you like, then fold the folded paper, then fold once more. This is all you are allowed to do. Then you may make just one straight scissor cut across the twice folded sheet.

Two answers are required. What is the maximum number of pieces you can obtain when you sort the two cut part out? How do you do the folding to get the maximum number of pieces? You have to do it in your head.

ANSWER:

23.11	Minutes allowed	10
	Time taken	
	Points gained	

REPLACEMENT

Replace the first letter in each pair of words either side of the brackets with another letter which will form two new English words. Then place this letter in the brackets. When you have completed this for all five pairs of words you will find another word reading downwards in the brackets. What is it?

WIND ( ) CAP
AVER ( ) BATH
MACE ( ) RACK
SATIN ( ) DEMON
TOUR ( ) LAWN

ANSWER:

23.12

Minutes allowed	10
Time taken	
Points gained	

WORD SEARCH

Five seven-lettered words have been hidden in this grid. They all have the same two-letter prefix which, for each word, has been omitted from the grid. The remaining letters for each word have been written downwards in the grid in random order. What are the five words?

E	I	O	R	O
U	A	V	D	I
I	S	E	E	L
S	T	S	G	S
V	N	L	I	H

ANSWER:

23.13

Minutes allowed	15
Time taken	
Points gained	

WORD WORK

Rearrange the letters below to make a ten-lettered word.

GONEISCOMR

ANSWER:

23.14	Minutes allowed	5
	Time taken	
	Points gained	

DIY CROSSWORD

The words down and across are given below, but you must decide where the blank squares are.

		T			T		
			O				
R				R			
						O	
E							E

R	L	O	T
I	I	U	O
F	V	T	O
E	E		

PROOF TOT   D   S
DISSENTED   E   E
NIP IDOLS   P   P
WEBS ROBE   U   A
IDLE RENT   T   R
SATURATED   I   A
T   B   B   O   S   T
E   I   R   W   E   E
N   T   E   E   D   D
S   E   D   D
E   S

23.15	Minutes allowed	**30**
	Time taken	
	Points gained	

ANSWERS

	Your Time	Time Allowed	Points Gained

23.1 Touch the end of one to the centre of the other. If they are attracted the touching end belongs to the magnet; if not, the touching centre belongs to the magnet. — 10 —

23.2 Be last, and put your key in the bowl with least keys in it. You will have an even chance of your bowl being chosen, and an improved chance thereafter if it is. — 5 —

23.3

L	A	C	K		P	A	T	E
A	G	O		A		S	O	D
V	E	N	E	R	A	T	E	D
A		S		C		E		Y
	V	E	X		P	R	Y	
C		R		F		O		A
R	E	V	E	R	S	I	N	G
A	R	E		Y		D	I	E
B	A	D	E		A	S	P	S

— 30 —

23.4 The way to settle tricky taxonomic problems is by use of a Venn or Euler diagram, like the one overleaf.

CARRIED FORWARD

445

ANSWERS

BROUGHT FORWARD

23.4 (cont)

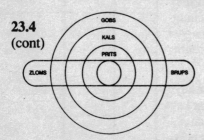

As will be seen, we can place a pencil point where a multi-racial creature will be in a rag-bag of categories falling into all of them. But there are zloms, brups and even gobs who have to subsist in exclusive isolation from other classes

15

23.5   72 hours, and they will show 6 o'clock when it is really 12 o'clock.

15

23.6   1. Starting from 22 you alternately subtract 2 and divide by 2.

10

23.7   The word is 'day', which comprises 2^7 x 3^3 x 5^2 seconds

20

CARRIED FORWARD

ANSWERS

BROUGHT FORWARD

23.8 There will be no change in proportion of boys and girls. The chance of any specific birth being male or female remains unchanged. The result would be that the birth rate would average less than 2 per women, less than enough to maintain to population.

15

23.9 The base is seven, and the numbers are • = 0, * = 1, ♥ = 2, ✦ = 3, ★ = 4, ✹ = 5, ✳ = 6

2 units 1 seven = 9	6 units = 6	6 units = 6
4 units = 4	0 units 1 seven = 7	3 units 1 seven = 10
1 unit 1 seven = 8	1 unit 1 seven = 8	5 units = 5

23.10 See answer overleaf

CARRIED FORWARD

ANSWERS

FOR CORRECT ANSWERS
Your   Time   Points
Time   Allowed | Gained

BROUGHT FORWARD

23.10

S	P	A	T		T	A	R	E
L	E	D		P		N	O	D
A	G	E		R	A	T	E	D
P		P		I				Y
	S	T	A	M	I	N	A	
R				E		E		A
I	N	T	E	R		W	I	G
D	O	E		S		E	R	E
S	T	E	P		E	L	K	S

30

23.11 You can get nine pieces. You fold three times the same way. Fold the paper to halve the length, halve what is now the width, fold the width again, and divide the width with your cut.

10

23.12 Holly

10

23.13 ABOLISH, ABSOLVE, ABRIDGE, ABSTAIN, ABUSIVE

15

23.14 Ergonomics

5

CARRIED FORWARD

ANSWERS

	FOR CORRECT ANSWERS		
	Your Time	Time Allowed	Points Gained

POINTS BROUGHT FORWARD

23.15 Answer below | | 30 |

TOTAL POINTS GAINED

CHAPTER SUMMARY

Chapter Handicap Total:

Correct Answers x 5 points:

Chapter Total:

Brought Forward:

Running Total:

CHAPTER
TWENTY FOUR

Target Time: 2 hours 46 minutes

MAJORITY ABOVE AVERAGE

THE GREAT MAJORITY ARE ABOVE THE AVERAGE. This statement may seem questionable. On most measurements about half the people are above average and about half are below it, but there are measurements on which the great majority of people are above average and only a small minority below it. Can you think of one?

Think it out! You will kick yourself, if you have to look up the answer.

ANSWER:

	Minutes allowed	5
24.1	Time taken	
	Points gained	

RAILWAY MYSTERY 1

The carriage axles on a train are solid, there is no differential as in a motor car. Yet with the outside wheel travelling further than the inside wheel when the train negotiates bends, there is no apparent slippage. How come?

ANSWER:

	Minutes allowed	5
24.2	Time taken	
	Points gained	

WAYS AND SUMS

Starting at the bottom left hand '7' move from circle to circle, either directly to the right or directly above, landing on nine numbers including the opening '7' and ending with the '9' in the top right hand corner. Add all nine numbers together to arrive at the total for the particular route chosen. How many different routes are there with a total of 43, and what is the lowest possible total?

ANSWER:

24.3

Minutes allowed	12
Time taken	
Points gained	

ANOTHER LOGICRACKER

Crack the logic found in the first two hexagons and apply it to the third to find the value of the question mark.

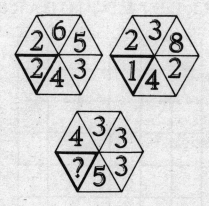

ANSWER:

24.4	Minutes allowed	6
	Time taken	
	Points gained	

POST THESE LETTERS

Place each of the following letters into the grid below in such a way that you can read six words across and the same six words downwards. The letters are: M V P I R H A R P L E T I O E T V D E E R R E E T V D T I O E A R P L E

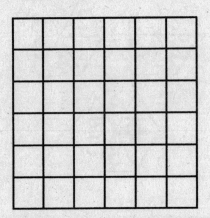

ANSWER:

24.5	Minutes allowed	15
	Time taken	
	Points gained	

REACH EIGHTEEN

How many ways can you score 18 on this dart-board? You have four darts each turn, but you can't use a combination of numbers in a different order once used.

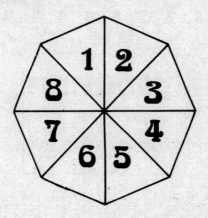

ANSWER:

24.6	Minutes allowed	6
	Time taken	
	Points gained	

GET ONE IN

Replace each question mark with one of the following digits in order that the calculation is correct.

1   2   2   3   4   4   7   9

$$(???/??x?)/?? = 1$$

ANSWER:

24.7	Minutes allowed	8
	Time taken	
	Points gained	

WHAT TIME?

Your clock was correct at midnight, but at that moment started to lose six minutes per hour. You look at the clock and see that it says 6 o'clock in the afternoon. You recall that you first realised that the clock has stopped exactly three and a half hours ago.

What is the correct time now?

ANSWER:

24.8	Minutes allowed	10
	Time taken	
	Points gained	

REVOLUTIONARY GEAR

Four cogs are in constant mesh as shown. Cog A has 100 teeth, cog B has 50 teeth, cog C has 20 teeth, while the smallest cog has only 15 teeth.

How many revolutions will cog C have to make before all four cogs have returned to exactly the same position as they are in now?

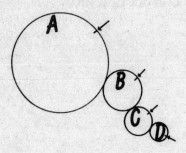

ANSWER:

24.9

Minutes allowed	10
Time taken	
Points gained	

A DOTTY PROBLEM

Look at this array of dots. How many squares of any size can be constructed from these dots where each corner of the squares rests on one of the dots in the array?

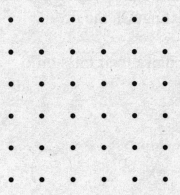

ANSWER:

24.10	Minutes allowed	12
	Time taken	
	Points gained	

LEAKY TANKER AGAIN!

A fire engine is travelling to a fire which is 45 miles away at a speed of 46mph. The engine holds 300 gallons of water but loses 150 gallons every hour through a small hole. They need 153 gallons to extinguish the fire.

Will they achieve their mission?

ANSWER:

24.11	Minutes allowed	10
	Time taken	
	Points gained	

NEW WORDS

Find the letter which can replace the third letter
in each pair of words to create two new words.
Place that letter in the brackets. When you have
done this for all eight pairs of words you will
discover an eight letter word reading downwards
in the brackets. What is it?

```
CATTLE  ( )  MARK
  LEAD  ( )  MOVED
  THAN  ( )  DRUNK
   ARE  ( )  DOPE
  CODA  ( )  RIB
  FOUL  ( )  COAL
  READ  ( )  BEST
  RACE  ( )  BAN
```

ANSWER:

24.12	Minutes allowed	10
	Time taken	
	Points gained	

TRAVEL TIME

The grid on the right represents a town plan with streets intersecting every half a mile. Four vehicles, A, B, C and D are travelling from one side of the town to another, following the routes indicated. A averaged 38mph, B averaged 25mph, C averaged 42mph and D averaged 49mph. Two of the vehicles arrived 'home' at exactly the same time. Which two were they, and how long did the journey take them?

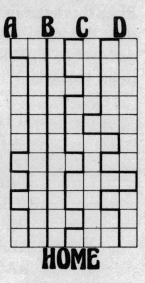

ANSWER:

24.13

Minutes allowed	12
Time taken	
Points gained	

PROFITABLE TRAVEL

En route from A to B you must travel from one square to any touching square, moving either directly upwards or to the right. When you have done this, add up all the numbers you have collected to find out the total for that particular route. What is the highest total possible for any one of the routes?

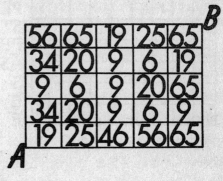

ANSWER:

24.14

Minutes allowed	15
Time taken	
Points gained	

DIY CROSSWORD

The words down and across are given below, but you must decide where the blank squares are.

S							S
		K					Y
				U			
S							R

INTER	LEI	E	R	D
EAR	GROPE	L	I	I
TOSS	ARC	O	C	S
PEP	PEER	P	K	U
STEM	OFF	E	S	S
PEA	SPRY			E
ASSUMES	A		A	D
S	R	P	G	F
E	A	E	E	A
E	T	R	S	R
	S	S	O	F	O
	P	L	P	E	R
	R	A	T	E	E
	Y	T			

ANSWERS

24.1 Some unfortunate people are amputees. There are not enough three-legged people to offset this, so the average number of legs per human being is just below two, although the vast majority have two. **5**

24.2 Trains present a conic surface to the rail. When the train goes round a bend, centrifugal force sends the carriages outwards so that the outer wheel climbs the cone towards the higher radius at the flange, while the inner wheel slides down to a lower radius. **5**

24.3 There are 2 routes to a score of 43, and the lowest total is 37. **12**

24.4 3. Starting with the top segment in each hexagon label them A to F clockwise. Then E equals $(((A \times D)/C) + F)/B$ **6**

CARRIED FORWARD

ANSWERS

	Your Time	Time Allowed	Points Gained
		BROUGHT FORWARD	
24.5	H A T T E R		
	A R R I V E		
	T R I P O D		
	T I P P L E		
	E V O L V E		
	R E D E E M	15	
24.6	24	6	
24.7	(342/19 x 4)/72 = 1	8	
24.8	11.30 pm	10	
24.9	15 revolutions	10	
24.10	105 (some are at a 45 degree angle)	12	
24.11	Yes, with 0.26087 of a gallon of water to spare	10	
24.12	SWIMMING	10	
24.13	Vehicles C and D, in a time of 12 min 51.43 sec	12	
24.14	369 (19+25+46+56+ 65+9+65+19+65)	15	
24.15	See answer overleaf		
		CARRIED FORWARD	

ANSWERS

CHAPTER SUMMARY

Chapter Handicap Total:

Correct Answers x 5 points:

Chapter Total:

Brought Forward:

Running Total:

CHAPTER
TWENTY FIVE

Target Time: 3 hours 25 minutes

RAILWAY MYSTERY 2

On every moving railway carriage there are metal parts which are travelling in the opposite direction to the train, and others which are travelling at twice the speed of the train. What are they?

ANSWER:

25.1	Minutes allowed	5
	Time taken	
	Points gained	

ANOTHER LOGICRACKER

Following the same logic as for the first three squares, what should replace the question mark in the final square?

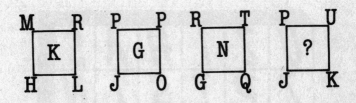

ANSWER:

	Minutes allowed	12
25.2	Time taken	
	Points gained	

UNRAVEL IT

Within the grid below is a coiled sentence. All of the letters of the sentence in an adjacent square, which can be touching by a full side or even by just a corner. Find the starting letter and unscramble the sentence.

U	Z	I	H	A	S
Z	P	T	S	I	N
L	E	Y	S	A	E

ANSWER:

25.3	Minutes allowed	12
	Time taken	
	Points gained	

SORTING PAIRS

The 28 numbers below belong to four distinct sets. Your problem is to sort them correctly. In each set there is a pair of 2-digit numbers and four functions of the pair, ie four results of arithmetic operations on the pair. Some numbers belong to more than one set, in such cases there will be duplicate copies of the functions. Your job is to discover the four original pairs of numbers. Here are the numbers and their four functions mixed and in rank order.

1,2,3,3,4,5,6,7,8,8,8
10,12,20,20,21,30,40,50,70,80
0.125, 0.3 recurring, 0.428571429, 0.8, 1.25, 2.3 recurring

ANSWER:

25.4	Minutes allowed	**20**
	Time taken	
	Points gained	

WHAT'S THE SENSE?

Following the same logic as for all the other
segments, can you work out which number
should replace the question mark?

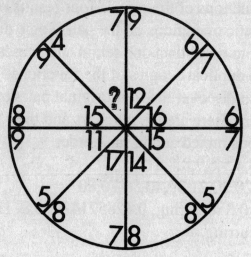

ANSWER:

25.5	Minutes allowed	12
	Time taken	
	Points gained	

REACH EIGHTEEN

The words down and across are given below, but you must decide where the blank squares are.

			O				W	
U								
	X						T	

```
UREA  PESO      O   S
EXTROVERT       B   W
THESE  SHE      T   E
TOO  IMPEL      R   E
OVERTONES       U   T
BENT  SOON      S   M
   E    E    O    H    I    E
   L    N    L    O    V    A
   O    S    E    B    E    T
   P    U    O    O
   E    E         T       E
        P    N    O    T   A
        U    E    T    S   S
        T    E    S        E
```

25.6	Minutes allowed	30
	Time taken	
	Points gained	

CODED KITCHEN TALK

Crack the code to reveal a well known saying:

AVV THUF JVVRZ ZWVPS AOL IYVAO

ANSWER:

25.7	Minutes allowed	15
	Time taken	
	Points gained	

BALANCING ACT

The top two sets of scales balance. How many of the third item are required to balance the third set?

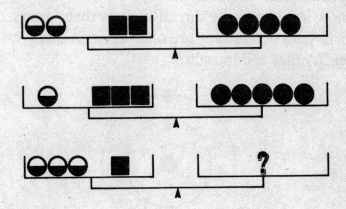

ANSWER:

25.8

Minutes allowed	5
Time taken	
Points gained	

ECLIPSE WATCH

Two planets are in orbit around the sun, as shown below. The inner planet takes eighteen years to complete one orbit, whilst the outer planet takes 45 years. If they both start moving now in a clockwise direction, how many years will pass before they are once again in line with each other and the sun?

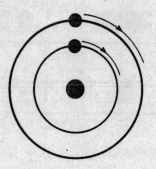

ANSWER:

25.9	Minutes allowed	10
	Time taken	
	Points gained	

SHOVE YA NUMBERS IN!

Complete the diagram below by placing one of the following numbers in each of the empty circles in such a way that each line vertically and horizontally totals 45. The numbers are: 11, 7, 7, 11, 7, 11, 18, 6, 2, 10, 10, 6, 2, 18, 11, 7

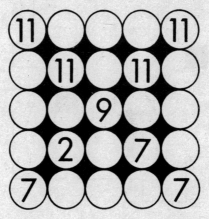

ANSWER:

25.10	Minutes allowed	12
	Time taken	
	Points gained	

T's TEASER

Using the black "T" shape, fill in the white area
of the diagram below. How many T's are
required in order that no gaps are left?

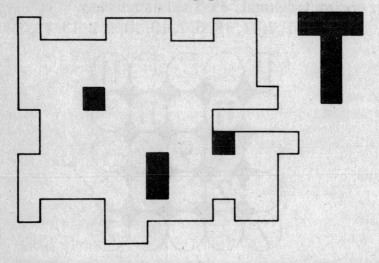

ANSWER:

25.11	Minutes allowed	12
	Time taken	
	Points gained	

SCORE A SCORE AND TWO

Start at any of the four corner numbers in this diagram, and work your way around the diagram following the black lines in such a way as to land on four further numbers. Add all five numbers together to obtain a total for that route. If you can only use one corner per route, how many different ways are there of reaching a total of 22?

ANSWER:

MORE DART SCORES

This new darts game has a different boards and set of rules from traditional darts. You have five darts each go and must score 27 with the five darts. You can land in any segment any number of times, but once a combination of segments has been used you cannot use it again in a different order. How many different ways are there of scoring 27 with five darts?

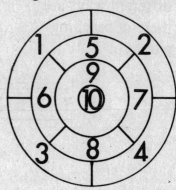

ANSWER:

25.13

Minutes allowed	15
Time taken	
Points gained	

AN AMBILOGICAL POSER

An ambilogical puzzle is logical in both ways, punlike. The letters below represent integer digits and the addition is correct in letters or their coded numbers. With the constraint that R = 2G, write down the equivalent of the sum in the hidden numerals.

```
   E I G H T
   T H R E E
     N I N E +
  _____
  T W E N T Y
```

ANSWER:

25.14	Minutes allowed	15
	Time taken	
	Points gained	

DIY CROSSWORD

The words down and across are given below, but
you must decide where the blank squares are.

V								
		B						
			M					
		N						
	X							

```
VOTED  INN     F  R
EXCELLENT      A  E
ALP ENDUE      V  P
UNTO  BEAT     O  R
FINANCIER      U  E
MERE  ONCE     R  S
I     T   N  C I  E
R     O   U  E T  N
A     N   D  L E  T
T     I   E  L
E     C   E  A
      N   D  B  M
      U   O  O  E
      T   E  N  N
```

	Minutes allowed	30
25.15	Time taken	
	Points gained	

ANSWERS

	Your Time	Time Allowed	Points Gained

FOR CORRECT ANSWERS

25.1 The part of the flange of the wheel which is below the rail must be going backwards. The ever changing point at the bottom of the wheel which is in contact must be still (momentarily) but the flange itself is going backwards. The top of each wheel is travelling (momentarily) at twice the speed of the train. — 5

25.2 P. Top two letters minus bottom two letters = middle letter — 12

25.3 "This is an easy puzzle" — 12

25.4 These are the pairs of factors: 1,8; 2,6; 3,7; 4,5 Where the first of each pair is 'a' and the second is 'b' the operations were: 10a, 10b, a/b, b/a, ab — 20

25.5 13. Total of outer numbers in segment = inner number in segment two along anti-clockwise — 12

CARRIED FORWARD

CHAPTER 25

ANSWERS

| | FOR CORRECT ANSWERS | | |
	Your Time	Time Allowed	Points Gained
BROUGHT FORWARD			

25.6

O	V	E	R	T	O	N	E	S
B		L		O		E		W
T	O	O		T	H	E	S	E
R		P	E	S	O			E
U	R	E	A		B	E	N	T
S				S	O	O	N	M
I	M	P	E	L		S	H	E
V		U		E		U		A
E	X	T	R	O	V	E	R	T

Time Allowed: 30

25.7 "Too many cooks spoil the broth" — 15

25.8 3 black circles — 5

25.9 15 years, on opposite sides of the sun — 10

25.10
11, 10, 11, 2, 11
10, 11, 11, 11, 2
11, 11, 9, 7, 7
 6, 7, 7, 7, 18
 7, 6, 7, 18, 7
— 12

25.11 15 T's — 12

25.12 5 routes total 22 — 12

25.13 102 ways — 15

CARRIED FORWARD

488

ANSWERS

| | FOR CORRECT ANSWERS | | |
| | Your Time | Time Allowed | Points Gained |

POINTS BROUGHT FORWARD

25.14

```
    8 5 2 9 1
    1 9 4 8 8
      3 5 3 8
  ─────────────
  1 0 8 3 1 7
```

| | | 15 |

25.15 See below

| | | 30 |

TOTAL POINTS GAINED

F	I	N	A	N	C	I	E	R
A		U		U		R		E
V	O	T	E	D		A	L	P
O			B	E	A	T		R
U	N	T	O		M	E	R	E
R		O	N	C	E			S
I	N	N		E	N	D	U	E
T		I		L		O		N
E	X	C	E	L	L	E	N	T

CHAPTER SUMMARY

Chapter Handicap Total:

Correct Answers x 5 points:

Chapter Total:

Brought Forward:

Running Total:

CHAPTER TWENTY SIX

Target Time: 4 hours 5 minutes

CHOOSING INGOTS

The gold ingots in the Boldovian Republic are cylindrical and to exaggerate their apparent value they are hollow. Unfortunately they are exactly the size that a solid cylinder of aluminium of the same weight would have. The practice of gold plating aluminium cylinders so as to make counterfeit ingots has arisen. You are offered some mixed ingots very cheap as an 'on inspection' bargain. You know that some are fakes. You may handle them but not scratch or injure them in any way. The gold is too thick to give a hollow ring. How do you sort out the gold ones?

ANSWER:

26.1	Minutes allowed	15
	Time taken	
	Points gained	

TARGET PRACTICE

Place one of the following numbers into each of the spaces in the target below in such a way that each segment of three numbers adds up to 156, and each circle of eight numbers adds up to 416.

49, 49, 50, 50,
51, 51, 51, 51,
51, 51, 52, 52,
52, 52, 52, 52,
53, 53, 53, 53,
54, 54, 56, 56.

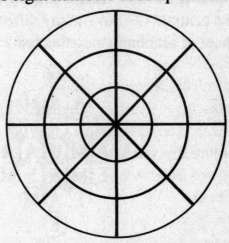

ANSWER:

26.2	Minutes allowed	**15**
	Time taken	
	Points gained	

HOW MANY GAMES?

Start at the central letter and make your way
around the diagram from circle to touching circle.
The object is to collect all the letters of the word
"GAME" in any order, but always starting from
the central "G". How many different ways are
there of accomplishing this task?

ANSWER:

26.3	Minutes allowed	12
	Time taken	
	Points gained	

FILL IT

After a hard day at work you need a refreshing bath. The hot tap will fill the bath in 27 minutes, if the plug is in, and the cold tap will fill the bath in 29 minutes under the same circumstances. If the bath is full and the taps are off it will take exactly 16 minutes for the bath to empty once the plug is removed.

How long will it take the bath to fill if the plug is left out and both taps are turned on?

ANSWER:

26.4	Minutes allowed	15
	Time taken	
	Points gained	

DECODE 'EM

The following four words have had all their letters mixed up. Can you unscramble them and say what the four words are?

1.   LATINSOODE

2.   SICAGROU

3.   AVERNEMUO

4.   ASKMERACHL

ANSWER:

26.5	Minutes allowed	**15**
	Time taken	
	Points gained	

MORE THAN ONE WAY

How many different routes are there from A to B following the arrows?

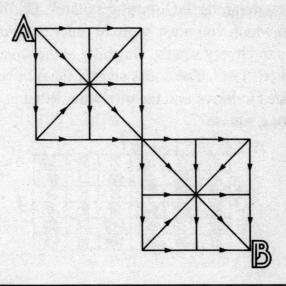

ANSWER:

26.6	Minutes allowed	20
	Time taken	
	Points gained	

HOW TO START

Obey the codes in each segment of the grid below, working backwards in order to find out which square is the "starting square", i.e. the one from which you must begin in order to land on each and every square, finishing at the square marked "last". The codes signify the number of squares to move and the direction. What is the starting square?

N

5S	1S	1SE	2S	5S	5W
1NE	1NE	4S	1NE	3S	4S
2E	1NE	1S	3S	1S	2N
3E	1NW	1SW	3N	1E	2N
3N	2E	3E	LAST	2N	5W
2N	2N	3NE	1NW	4N	4W

W   **E**

S

ANSWER:

26.7	Minutes allowed	15
	Time taken	
	Points gained	

FOUR CARS

Four cars are on their way home through a town in which the streets intersect every ³/4 mile. The route which each car followed is shown on the town plan on the right by a heavy black line. Car A travels at an average speed of 30mph, car B at 25mph, car C at 35mph and car D at 41mph. Which car will reach home first, and how far ahead of the second car will it be?

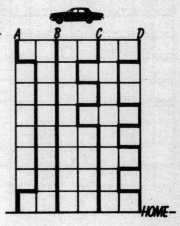

ANSWER:

26.8

Minutes allowed	12
Time taken	
Points gained	

DIY CROSSWORD

The words down and across are given below, but you must decide where the blank squares are.

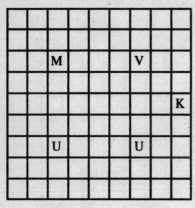

TREK	ROSE	S C
CATHARSIS		L O
VIA	AMUSE	A L
LAMAS	GNU	C L
EAGERNESS		K E
TAPE	EASE	N A
S	S	A	P	E G
T	E	L	A	S U
U	V	S	I	S E
U	E	O	R	
G	R	S	A	
U	T	T	A	R
S	A	E	R	
E	M	M	A	

26.9	Minutes allowed	30
	Time taken	
	Points gained	

ZIGGURAT

Each horizontal line of squares in the grid below must contain a word, and each square in a vertical line must contain the same letter as the other squares in its column. Four of the letters used are S, E, P and D. Using these four and another three letters, complete the grid.

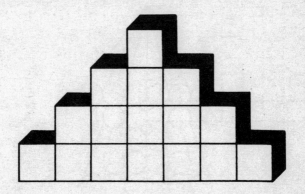

ANSWER:

26.10

Minutes allowed	6
Time taken	
Points gained	

SHRINK – GROW

Each horizontal line of circles must contain a word, and each circle in a vertical line must contain the same letter as other circles directly above or below it, i.e. this does not apply where there are gaps in the vertical line. Four of the letters are T, S, A and O. Complete the grid.

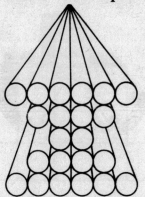

ANSWER:

26.11	Minutes allowed	15
	Time taken	
	Points gained	

THE INS AND OUTS OF IT

The outer numbers in the diagram have something to do with the inner numbers. Which number is missing from the inner set?

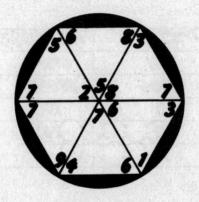

ANSWER:

26.12

Minutes allowed	10
Time taken	
Points gained	

WHAT IS THE RULE?

In this diagram you can see what a computer program has done to various numbers. What would the output be if the input were "1"?

INPUT	OUTPUT
111	61675
1000	500007
5	195
12	79
1	

ANSWER:

26.13	Minutes allowed	20
	Time taken	
	Points gained	

QUIZ

1. What carries signals from the eye to the brain?

2. What is the name of the ship of the underwater explorer, Jacques Cousteau?

3. What type of tree yields conkers?

4. From which kind of wood was the 'Kon-Tiki' raft made?

5. What is a woofer?

6. What is a dipsomaniac?

7. What is the fruit of a rosebush called?

8. Is a spider an insect?

9. What is a baby eagle called?

10. What imaginary line encircles the earth?

11. How many wings has a bee?

12. What was the name of the mission that landed the first men on the moon?

26.14	Minutes allowed	15
	Time taken	
	Points gained	

DIY CROSSWORD

The words down and across are given below, but you must decide where the blank squares are.

								D
				A				
			O		T			
				P				
	K							

SEPARATOR	D	D
TIER OPEN	E	E
TARTS GAY	S	C
DESCRIBED	T	I
COT OKAPI	R	D
DODO ELAN	O	U
I S L R	Y	O
N A O O	E	U
G T O T	R	S
O E P A		
T D A P		
B A N I		
A S T E		
R P E R		

26.15	Minutes allowed	▶ 30
	Time taken	
	Points gained	

ANSWERS

	Your Time	Time Allowed	Points Gained
26.1 The two cylinders will have different moments of inertia. You make a short slope on a smooth table or floor, roll the ingots down and choose those that roll furthest.		15	
26.2		15	
26.3 There are 13 ways		12	
26.4 1 hour, 50 min, 52 secs		15	
26.5 1. Desolation 2. Gracious 3. Manoeuvre 4. Ramshackle		15	
26.6 289 (hands up those who counted them, and those who multiplied 17 by 17)		20	
26.7 The starting square is the one marked '1NE' on the third row down		15	

26.2

CARRIED FORWARD

ANSWERS

FOR CORRECT ANSWERS

Your Time	Time Allowed	Points Gained

BROUGHT FORWARD

26.8 Car B will arrive first, 36 seconds ahead of car A — 12

26.9

C	A	T	H	A	R	S	I	S
O		A		L		E		L
L	A	M	A	S		V	I	A
L			R	O	S	E		C
E	A	S	E		T	R	E	K
A		T	A	P	E			N
G	N	U		A	M	U	S	E
U		N		I		S		S
E	A	G	E	R	N	E	S	S

30

26.10

A
R A P
C R A P E
S C R A P E D — 6

26.11

S T O R E D
T O R E
O R
C O R N
A C O R N — 15

26.12 **5.** Two outer numbers = twice inner number in opposite segment — 10

CARRIED FORWARD

ANSWERS

POINTS BROUGHT FORWARD

26.13 7.5 (Output = (Input x
Input + 14) ÷ 2   20

26.14 1. The optic nerve
2. The Calypso
3. The horse chestnut
4. Balsa wood 5. A low-
frequency speaker
6. An alcohol addict
7. The hip 8. No
9. An eaglet
10. The equator
11. Four
12. Apollo 11   15

26.15

D	E	S	C	R	I	B	E	D
E		A		O		A		E
C	O	T		T	A	R	T	S
I		E	L	A	N			T
D	O	D	O		T	I	E	R
U			O	P	E	N		O
O	K	A	P	I		G	A	Y
U		S		E		O		E
S	E	P	A	R	A	T	O	R

30

TOTAL POINTS GAINED

CHAPTER SUMMARY

Chapter Handicap Total:

Correct Answers x 5 points:

Chapter Total:

    Brought Forward:

Running Total:

CHAPTER
TWENTY SEVEN

Target Time: 3 hours 13 minutes

TIME ZONES

Marjory was talking by telephone to Alfred:

Alfred: I will have to check up and call you back. Where are you?

Marjory: I may not tell you. I'll call you.

Alfred: It is midnight here. What time zone are you in?

Marjory: I cannot tell you. No one could.

Alfred: Come on! You are not in space. On earth the time zones cover every point.

Marjory: I am on earth, in one place, but I am not in a time zone, nor between two time zones.

Where is Marjory?

ANSWER:

	Minutes allowed	10
27.1	Time taken	
	Points gained	

WHERE ON EARTH?

Here are the outlines of five British counties.
Match the letter with the county name.

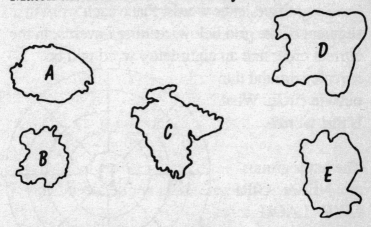

LINCOLNSHIRE NORFOLK SHROPSHIRE
DEVON   GRAMPIAN

ANSWER:

27.2	Minutes allowed	15
	Time taken	
	Points gained	

UNSCRAMBLE

Unscramble the eight groups of four letters below so that when placed in front of the letter D they form eight five-letter words. Place each word in a segment of the grid below, reading inwards, in the correct order and an eight-letter word will be revealed around the outside circle. What is that word?

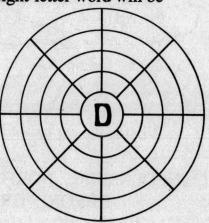

The letter groups are: NELA GIRI
LIYE LAOU
NOUF DINU
NARB URNO

ANSWER:

27.3	Minutes allowed	12
	Time taken	
	Points gained	

A MONTH TO ANSWER

Answer the following questions and place the first letter of each answer in the respective squares in the grid below. What word is created?

1. Which planet is called the "Red Planet"?
2. Which fruit can be placed in front of "Jack" to create a spirit drink?
3. What is the four-lettered currency of South Africa?
4. What is the northernmost point of mainland Australia?
5. What is the capital of Finland?

1	2	3	4	5

ANSWER:

27.4	Minutes allowed	9
	Time taken	
	Points gained	

FIND THE WANDERERS

Starting at the bottom left hand "W" and working your way from square to touching square either upwards or to the right until you reach the top right hand "S", you will always land on nine squares. How many different routes will enable you to land on all the letters of the word "WANDERERS"?

ANSWER:

27.5	Minutes allowed	15
	Time taken	
	Points gained	

MORE FREEBIES

You have won a shopping spree in your local shopping arcade, which comprises 13 shops laid out as shown. Each circle represents a shop and the figure indicates the number of minutes you are allowed in that shop during your spree. You are permitted to visit a total of five shops, starting from, and only including, one corner shop. What is the maximum time that you can spend on your spree?

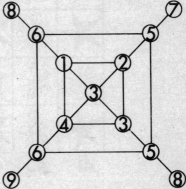

ANSWER:

27.6	Minutes allowed	6
	Time taken	
	Points gained	

SYMBOL SOLVE

Each like symbol in this diagram has the same value. The numbers next to the rows and columns represent the totals for the four shapes in that row or column. What is the missing total?

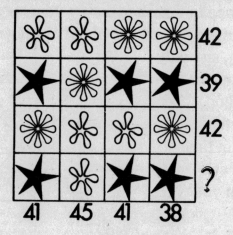

42
39
42
?

41 45 41 38

ANSWER:

27.7

Minutes allowed	6
Time taken	
Points gained	

NOT ANOTHER BOARD!

Here is a new-style dartboard, on which you must score 25 with three darts. You can land in any segment any number of times, but once a combination of three segments has been used it cannot be reused in a different order. How many ways are there of scoring 25?

ANSWER:

27.8

Minutes allowed	6
Time taken	
Points gained	

DIY CROSSWORD

The words down and across are given below, but you must decide where the blank squares are.

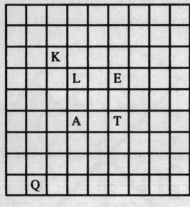

ELSE	EATS		R	S
RELIGIOUS			E	W
TRADE	SUE		I	E
SIFT	SIDE		N	E
EQUIPMENT			S	T
IRK	AVERT		T	M
L	I	A	G	A	T	E
I	S	T	U	T	A
K	S	O	T	E	T
E	U	P	S
D	E	R	L
O	E	E	E
V	M	S	E
A	U	T	R

ELSE EATS R S
RELIGIOUS E W
TRADE SUE I E
SIFT SIDE N E
EQUIPMENT S T
IRK AVERT T M
L I A G A T E
I S T U T A
K S O T E T
E U P S
D E R L
O E E E
V M S E
A U T R

27.9	Minutes allowed	30
	Time taken	
	Points gained	

TWENTY FIVE

Each row and column of five numbers should total twenty five. Simply calculate the eight missing numbers, and add them together to obtain the answer to this puzzle.

6		5		6
	5	5		
6	5		3	2
4		3	3	7
	7	3	6	2

ANSWER:

27.10

Minutes allowed	6
Time taken	
Points gained	

MAKE OR BREAK

Which of the cubes, A to F, can be constructed
from the flattened out cube shown?

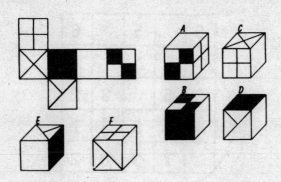

ANSWER:

27.11	Minutes allowed	12
	Time taken	
	Points gained	

ROUND FIELD

You have a field which is circular and has a radius of 5km. You want to place a rope around the field which is 100 metres out from the edge all the way round. How long will the rope have to be?

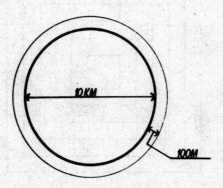

10 KM

100M

ANSWER:

27.12

Minutes allowed	15
Time taken	
Points gained	

2-WAY MAZE

Which two entries will allow you to take routes that will lead you to the centre of the maze?

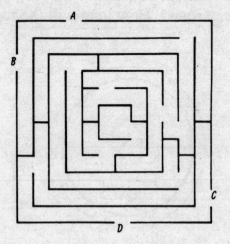

ANSWER:

27.13	Minutes allowed	3
	Time taken	
	Points gained	

SAME SPACE

There are two pairs of shapes of equal area in the diagram below. What are the two pairs?

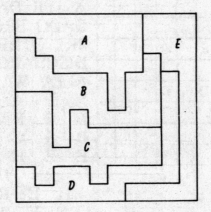

ANSWER:

27.14	Minutes allowed	18
	Time taken	
	Points gained	

DIY CROSSWORD

The words down and across are given below, but you must decide where the blank squares are.

W									
			R		O				
			D		D				

WEIRDNESS   S W
ALTER   DAB   E   I
DADO   ERGO   R   D
SKI   OTHER   I   O
DISCHARGE   A   W
ALFA   WADI   L   H
I   L   A   L   I   O
M   O   R   O   S   O
B   S   C   A   E   D
E   E   H   D
D   R   D   R
H   E   D   R   I
A   F   R   I   D
S   T   A   G   E
D   E

Minutes allowed	30
Time taken	
Points gained	

27.15

526

ANSWERS

	FOR CORRECT ANSWERS		
	Your Time	Time Allowed	Points Gained

27.1 Marjory was exactly at the North Pole, where all the time zones meet. She was neither in a *single* time zone nor *between two* but in *all* of them. In practice, GMT prevails at the poles. — 10

27.2 A = Norfolk
B = Shropshire
C = Devon,
D = Grampian
E = Lincolnshire — 15

27.3 FEBRUARY (Found, Eland, Brand, Rigid, Undid, Aloud, Round, Yield) — 12

27.4 MARCH (Mars, Apple, Rand, Cape York, Helsinki) — 9

27.5 There are 6 routes by which you can collect all the letters of "Wanderers" — 15

27.6 31 minutes — 6

27.7 42 — 6

27.8 There are 6 ways of scoring 25 — 6

CARRIED FORWARD

ANSWERS

FOR CORRECT ANSWERS
Your   Time   Points
Time   Allowed Gained

BROUGHT FORWARD

27.9

R	E	L	I	G	I	O	U	S
E		I		U		V		W
I	R	K		T	R	A	D	E
N		E	L	S	E			E
S	I	D	E		S	I	F	T
T		E	A	T	S			M
A	V	E	R	T		S	U	E
T		M		O		U		A
E	Q	U	I	P	M	E	N	T

    30

27.10 47   **6**

27.11 A, D and E   **12**

27.12 31.73 km   **15**

27.13 D and C   **3**

27.14 B and C; D and E   **18**

27.15 See overleaf

ANSWERS

FOR CORRECT ANSWERS

Your Time	Time Allowed	Points Gained

POINTS BROUGHT FORWARD

27.15 Answer below | | 30

TOTAL POINTS GAINED

CHAPTER SUMMARY

Chapter Handicap Total:

Correct Answers x 5 points:

Chapter Total:

Brought Forward:

Running Total:

CHAPTER
TWENTY EIGHT

Target Time: 4 hours 25 minutes

WALK IN FREE FALL

You are in free fall orbit in a large chamber as shown. The walls are of iron except the one at the bottom of the illustration. You have to walk with your magnetic boots from corner A to corner B, by the shortest route where your boots can hold to the surface. How long is your magnetic stroll?

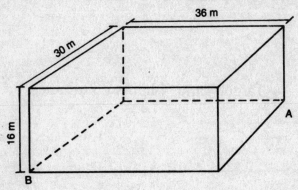

ANSWER:

28.1	Minutes allowed	15
	Time taken	
	Points gained	

TWO VIEWS

Here are two elevations of the same object. Draw the plan.

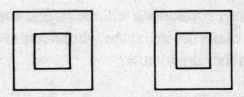

ANSWER:

28.2	Minutes allowed	10
	Time taken	
	Points gained	

COGITATE IN GEAR

Four cog wheels are in constant mesh as shown in the diagram. Cog A has 80 teeth, cog B 40 teeth, cog C 25 teeth and cog D, the smallest, 12 teeth. How many revolutions will the largest cog wheel have to make before all the wheels return to the position they are in now?

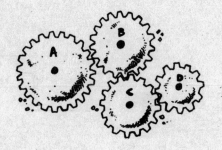

ANSWER:

28.3

Minutes allowed	15
Time taken	
Points gained	

FIT THE BLACK

How many times will the black shape on the right fit into the white area (ie excluding the black rectangle) in the diagram below, so as to completely fill it?

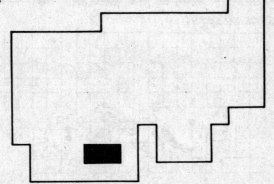

ANSWER:

28.4

Minutes allowed	15
Time taken	
Points gained	

MAKE-UP

All of the larger shapes numbered 1 to 4 can be
created using a combination of shapes A to F.
The smaller shapes may be used a maximum of
twice each in forming each of the larger shapes.
Which smaller shapes are used to form each of
the larger shapes?

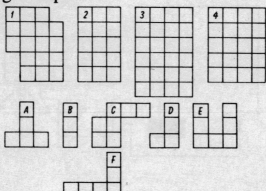

ANSWER:

28.5	Minutes allowed	12
	Time taken	
	Points gained	

SPIDER PUZZLE

A trainee web maker at the St John the Arachnid College of Higher Education has come up with this effort. He now, as part of his final exam, has to work out how many ways there are of travelling from A to B following the arrows. What is the answer?

ANSWER:

28.6	Minutes allowed	24
	Time taken	
	Points gained	

A HUNDRED LINES

Place each of the following numbers into the circles in the diagram in such a way that each row and clumn of five numbers has a total of 100. The numbers to use are:

21, 8, 19, 20, 5,
21, 21, 22, 35,
19, 37, 4, 19, 21,
8, 17, 18, 23, 19,
19, 21, 32, 19,
21 and 31.

ANSWER:

<table>
<tr><td rowspan="3">28.7</td><td>Minutes allowed</td><td>15</td></tr>
<tr><td>Time taken</td><td></td></tr>
<tr><td>Points gained</td><td></td></tr>
</table>

FIND THE SENTENCE

This diagram presents a code written in a clockwise direction, starting with the highlighted circle. What does it read?

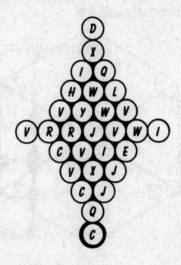

ANSWER:

	Minutes allowed	15
28.8	Time taken	
	Points gained	

LOGIC LINKS

Work out the logic that links all of the segments
in the diagram and thus work out what should
replace the question mark.

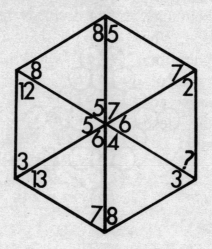

ANSWER:

28.9	Minutes allowed	30
	Time taken	
	Points gained	

HIGH LOW

Starting from one of the corners and following the thin black lines you must collect 5 numbers. Only one corner can be included and you cannot retrace your steps. Having collected 5 numbers you add them together and divide by seven to obtain a total. What are the highest total and the lowest total that can be scored by following these instructions?

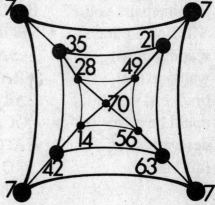

ANSWER:

28.10	Minutes allowed	21
	Time taken	
	Points gained	

HIDDEN THEME

For each pair of words find the letter which can
replace the intitial letter in the left hand word
and also be inserted before the right hand word.
Place that letter in the brackets, and when you
have done this for
all nine pairs you   HARSH ( ) ARCH
will find a phrase   UNBORN ( ) ON
reading down-   SAIL ( ) ONE
wards in the   RAFT ( ) ANGER
brackets, which   EARTH ( ) LOVE
could be a   OCHE ( ) CUTE
description of   CATCH ( ) ORAL
this book!   OAT ( ) LAND
   MUCH ( ) ABLE

ANSWER:

28.11

Minutes allowed	15
Time taken	
Points gained	

SPEED QUIZ

ANSWERS

1. What is the voltage of most car batteries?

2. Does Uranus have rings?

3. Which sense is most closely linked to memory?

4. What is it impossible to keep open if you sneeze?

5. What is meant by hirsute?

6. Which constellation contains the stars Castor and Pollux?

7. Which season begins with the vernal equinox?

8. What is a limestone pillar rising from the floor of a cave called?

9. What is the hardest gem?

10. Of which family of trees is the sycamore a member?

11. Who invented the railway sleeping car in 1859?

12. What is the name of the South American ostrich-like bird?

28.12	Minutes allowed	15
	Time taken	
	Points gained	

MAKE IT ADD UP

Place one of the following numbers into each vacant square in the diagram, so that each line of five numbers totals 55. The numbers to use are: 22, 22, 16, 16, 15, 15, 11, 6, 6, 5, 5, 2 and 2.

		16		16
		16	16	
16	16	11	6	6
	6	6		
6		6		6

ANSWER:

28.13

Minutes allowed	15
Time taken	
Points gained	

LAND, SLIP

Starting at the central 'S' on each occasion move from circle to touching circle in order to land on each of the letters of the word SLIP. On each move you can only land on four letters, including the intitial S, but the order of the other three letters is unimportant. How many different ways are there of landing on all of the letters of the word SLIP?

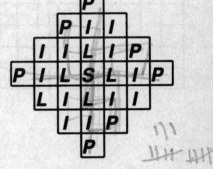

ANSWER:

<table>
<tr><td rowspan="3">28.14</td><td>Minutes allowed</td><td>18</td></tr>
<tr><td>Time taken</td><td></td></tr>
<tr><td>Points gained</td><td></td></tr>
</table>

DIY CROSSWORD

The words down and across are given below, but you must decide where the blank squares are.

```
ERA  RIDES     F  D
FARMSTEAD      I  I
EVIL  BOYO     R  S
ARCHED RAP     E  L
DESPERATE      B  O
LOGO  LISP     R  C
O    R    I    I    A  A
P    O    L    D    N  T
E    P    L    L    D  E
R    E    S    E       E
A    Y    S    V
     H    E    A    O
     I    N    R    L
     S    D    I    E
```

	Minutes allowed	30
28.15	Time taken	
	Points gained	

546

ANSWERS

28.1 The chamber when opened up would look like the drawing below, and you would follow the path shown. Using Pythagoras the distance is the square root of $(36+16)^2 + (30+16)^2$ = 69.426219 metres

28.2 There are two possibilities. The best answer is both, giving a bonus point, but either will do.

15

10

CARRIED FORWARD

ANSWERS

	Your Time	Time Allowed	Points Gained
BROUGHT FORWARD			
28.3 15 revolutions		15	
28.4 17 times		15	
28.5 1. D, E and F 2. A, B and E 3. A, B, B, E and F 4. B, C, D and F		12	
28.6 There are 17 routes		24	
28.7 21 31 21 04 23 32 21 21 21 05 22 21 20 19 18 08 19 19 19 35 17 08 19 37 19		15	
28.8 "Mensa members have the biggest"		15	
28.9 The missing figure is 13. The two numbers on the leading edge of each segment, reading anti-clockwise, are totalled to give the remaining figure in the segment two ahead		30	

CARRIED FORWARD

ANSWERS

FOR CORRECT ANSWERS

	Your Time	Time Allowed	Points Gained

BROUGHT FORWARD

28.10 The highest possible total is 35, the lowest is 15 — 21

28.11 "MIND GAMES" — 15

28.12
1. Twelve volts
2. Yes
3. Smell
4. The eyes
5. Hairy
6. Gemini
7. Spring
8. Stalagmite
9. Diamond
10. The maple family
11. George M. Pullman
12. Rhea — 15

28.13
16 2 16 5 16
 2 16 16 16 5
16 16 11 6 6
15 6 6 6 22
 6 15 6 22 6 — 15

28.14 There are 10 routes — 18

28.15 See answer overleaf

CARRIED FORWARD

ANSWERS

FOR CORRECT ANSWERS

	Your Time	Time Allowed	Points Gained

POINTS BROUGHT FORWARD

28.15 Answer below | | 30 | |

TOTAL POINTS GAINED

F	A	R	M	S	T	E	A	D
I		O		A		N		I
R	A	P		R	I	D	E	S
E		E	V	I	L			L
B	O	Y	O		L	O	G	O
R			L	I	S	P		C
A	C	H	E	D		E	R	A
N		I		L		R		T
D	E	S	P	E	R	A	T	E

CHAPTER SUMMARY

Chapter Handicap Total:

Correct Answers x 5 points:

Chapter Total:

Brought Forward:

Running Total: